Crisis of Political & Religious Conflict in Southern Thailand

Written by
Dr. Sompong Daney Dumdeang

Copyright © 2025 Dr. Daney Dumdeang

All rights reserved.

ISBN: 979-8-89324-935-4

No part of this book may be reproduced, stored in a retrieval system, or transmitted in any form or by any means—electronic, mechanical, photocopying, recording, or otherwise—without prior written permission of the publisher, except for brief quotations used in reviews or articles.

The opinions expressed by the Author are not necessarily those held by the Publishers.

The information contained within this book is strictly for informational purposes. The material may include information, products, or services by third parties. As such, the Author and Publisher do not assume responsibility or liability for any third-party material or opinions. The publisher is not responsible for websites (or their content) that are not owned by the publisher. Readers are advised to do their own due diligence when it comes to making decisions.

Published by Franklin Publishers

Printed in the United States of America

For permissions, inquiries, or additional copies, contact:

Franklin Publishers

www.franklinpublishers.com

Crisis...Conflict The Three Southern Border Provinces

Dr. Sompong Dumdeang

Intrakieat Rodpradit

Dedication

"This book is dedicated to Pipat Dumdeang

And his fallen comrade, Phi Khiang Chantarat…

Who were brutally murdered.

Both of them were victims of the violence in the three southern border provinces."

Pipat Dumdeang

Pipat Dumdeang, headmaster of Pattana Suksa School of Nongchic District, Pattani province, was born on 13th 2042 at Moo 4, Ranot District, Songkhla Province, has 10 brothers and sisters of the same blood, and the author is 3rd person of 10 brothers and sisters.

Pipat was an elementary school student at Wat Pang Tri, Rawa district, Songkhla Province. Because of his excellent ability, he was able to graduate from elementary school, which is a 4-year curriculum that he was able to pass within 3 years.

After graduating from Mathayom 6 at that time, he went to study at Teacher's College and took his career as a teacher for all of his life. He has intelligent ability, obtained a higher certificate of Education (Por Mor) under the curriculum of the Ministry of Education and later studied at Prince of Songkhla University (twilight programme) and graduated Bachelor of Science in Education from that University.

Pattana Suksa School, where he was headmaster, was located in a remote area of Pattani province, and most of his students were Muslim. Pipat was a teacher who devoted his life to teaching his students with a great heart, determined to give them education and provide them with a more prospected future in life. And he loves his students without prejudice, whether most of his students have different beliefs in religion.

Being appointed as the headmaster of that school was considered a successful young adult civil servant in Pattani Province. In this area, people have different opinions and different beliefs resulting from history.

Pipat Dumdeang has been trusted by security agencies to help support the government's work in the security field in the southern area had closely cooperated with the then Gen.Sant Chitpatima, Commander of the 4th Regional of Thai Army.

Pipat Dumdeang and his close friend, Kiang Chantarat, were brutally murdered in broad daylight while riding on a motorcycle into downtown in front of the eyes of many people after meeting with a high-ranking military.

Question: Why was Teacher Pipat killed so brutally?

Teacher Pipat Dumdeang was brutally murdered and burned alive together with his best friend, Phi Kiang Jantrat, while riding a motorbike in the back of a motorcycle through a market in the middle of the day.

They were both victims of conflict.

It can be said that the motive for Teacher Pipat's brutal murder was the result of

From the historical, ideological conflict, the dissidents see that Khru Pipat is a representative of the government and a key man working with the state's security forces, thus creating distrust in the dissidents. Pol. Lt. Col. Charuek Sam-angsri, who the author calls Aoi Kloe, has given an interesting opinion about Khru Pipat being brutally murdered. "The murder of Khru Pipat Dumdeang was a murder that the villagers

knew was a political murder, a scapegoat murder, which the foreigners called "scapegoat," as the author and co-author argued about the story of the conflict in the three southern border provinces when the author's and co-author's friends traveled to visit the author at

Portland, Oregon, United States, September to October 2014

The author's friend is a sergeant-level border patrol policeman. A sergeant-level border patrol policeman is considered a senior police officer. He has served as a commissioned officer for the Border Patrol Police throughout his life. The area of responsibility is in the South. Therefore, he was aware of the incident in detail. He mentioned the reason why Khru Phiphat was killed because: Teacher Pipat was involved with the security forces, and the terrorists found out that the high-ranking military officers had been visiting Teacher Pipat all the time, which made them distrust Teacher Pipat. No matter how much good deeds Teacher Pipat did, the terrorists did not trust him, which resulted in Teacher Pipat being killed."

Khru Phiphat, the author's elder brother, is a great loss for the Dumdeang family. It is a great loss for the education sector of Pattani Province, affecting the national education sector and also the loss of an important person who served as a security force along with the military.

The loss of Khru Phiphat, the author's elder brother, was a great loss for the Dumdeang family and a loss for the nation's publisher, who had created only good deeds for the South, society, and the country. This is a good example of conflicts in the three southern border provinces. With deepest regret, the author vows to investigate what caused the conflict that has occurred for decades to find a solution to the conflict as a way to repay the kindness of the author's homeland.

The author has, therefore, conducted research with fellow authors on the conflict problem for decades. The book "The Crisis of Conflict in the Three Southern Border Provinces," which is now in the hands of the reader, is the answer that both of us would like to give to the reader and the suggestions that the government should use as a guideline for resolving the conflict problem in the three southern border provinces.

We both writers agree with a pacifist who said,

"I do not agree with the use of violence in any form, but I firmly believe in resolving conflicts peacefully through negotiation."

We both writers believe that the deaths of Khru Pipat Dumdeang and Kiang Chanrat will not be in vain.

To Teacher Pipat Dumdeang

The sound of the thunder crashed down.
Grasping for air, lacking spirit
Black, scary, dark
Life has come to an end.

Oh, how sad, how disheartened
Lonely, dazed, confused
Behind is still jealous and concerned
Does anyone give me some kindness?

Khet Tai for the nation, religion and king
For the state, my dear, provide
Never give up. Never give up.
Must be defeated by the evil and unjust.

Reward for good deeds
The remains behind are still enormous.
Do good and have immediate results.
Good, the Dhamma is very profound.

Go, go well, be happy.
Don't be sad, don't be jealous, don't be so worried.
Cut off anger, cut off greed, cut off love.
Stop, kill, and grind.

The sound of heavenly conch shells
Arrived, the most exquisite dream
Happiness, goodness, eternal
Heaven remains on earth, wandering…

Teachers of Hong Chik District, Pattani Province

Phatthanasuksa School, Nong Chik District, Pattani Province

Note: When Khru Piu Pat was the head teacher, most of the students were Muslims.

Author Praise

Statement of Congratulations

The stories you have presented in every thread have made me, the reader, understand the causes of conflict in the three southern border provinces and the ways to resolve conflicts. I have seen many ideas from scholars to resolve the problem. However, for the readers, I would like to present the solutions to the problems in the three southern provinces using the Buddhist method as follows:

The Buddha said that to successfully resolve any problem, four principles must be used:

1. Study the problem thoroughly

2. Study the cause of the problem and its related factors

3. To understand how to solve the problem

4. The way to solve the problem

(Suffering, the cause of suffering, means of extinction and ways and means how to solve said problems)

Readers who are the same locals as the writer can understand the feelings of their friends who are aware of the problems of their hometowns very well. On this occasion, I would like to pay my respects to those who have passed away from this incident.

I would like to take this opportunity to express my gratitude to the author.

Best regards

Professor Boonlert Nokkaew

Independent Scholar

Acknowledgments

Thank you, Patty Dumdeang

Patty is the writer's beloved wife. She is not only a woman of spiritual beauty but also a woman of beauty and charm. She is a former Miss Montana from the United States. She was a student while the writer was a lecturer at Washington University. Later, she became the writer's wife. She is the writer's soulmate who shares both the hardships and the happiness. The author has been writing for over 40 years. She is a gentle but strong-minded wife. She is brave enough to accept the dangers of the author as her husband. She went to do field research in the southern border provinces. She supported and encouraged the author wholeheartedly because she knew that the author had the spirit to work to help the people in the South. She supported the author, and the author worked together to make this book. The mission was successfully completed.

She has also been a professor of English at a U.S. university for over 25 years. She played a major role in helping the author with the English language in this book. The author is lucky to have her as his life partner. She is the most wonderful mother to three children and seven grandchildren.

Thank you, Pol. Lt. Col. Jaruk Sam-ang Sri.

Pol. Lt. Col. Jaruek Sam-angsri, a childhood friend and close relative of the author, used to help the author by driving him to high-risk areas while the author was conducting field research in the southern border provinces. He was a high-ranking border patrol police officer who mostly worked in the southern border provinces until his retirement. He, therefore, had a lot of first-hand experience in the unrest in the three southern border provinces. Therefore, his information is very useful for both of us writers.

He also traveled to visit the author in the United States twice. The last time, he traveled to America for two purposes: to seek treatment because he had been ill with many diseases for a long time; and to visit the author himself, traveling with Intarakiat Rodpradit, the co-author of this book. Therefore, I am one of the people who have participated in providing the correct information and helping both writers with sincerity.

This made us able to write this book successfully.

Thank you Int Kiet Rodpradit

Intarakiat Rodpradit is a co-author of this book. The author feels a deep debt of gratitude to him, especially during the latter part of working on this important piece. From August to September 2015, he devoted a lot of time to writing this book. He is a diligent person. He is a man who sticks to his promise. I have worked with people from many walks of life, from the White House to every level of the judiciary in the United States. I have never met someone as honest and hardworking as Intarakiat. I consider him a great asset to have chosen him as a co-author.

Thai Because of the long gap of decades, the Thai language of the writer has become stale. The writer is lucky to have him as a co-writer, and both of us are lucky to have worked together for the benefit of our southern people and for the Thai people, both nationally and for the peace and happiness of the world.

The author would like to thank Lukdet for designing the book beautifully and deeply expressing the meaning.

Foreword I

I, the author, deeply thank Franklin Publishers for assisting in the republication of this work and shedding light on the crisis in Southern Thailand in the English language for a worldwide audience.

This book, both a phenomenon and a critical effort, is the most important and masterful work of my life. I lost my older brother due to the weak, misleading, and unjust treatment inflicted by the Thai government over many decades. In my pursuit of truth, I nearly lost my own life conducting research and placing myself in dangerous, even deadly situations, to uncover and document the root causes of the conflict in Southern Thailand.

I am proud to present this important and meaningful book in both Thai and English. It speaks for itself. The information contained within is powerful, so powerful that some authorities may find it uncomfortable. But truth cannot be silenced.

This book is my life. I am fighting for the southerners to regain their freedom, as I myself am a native of Southern Thailand. I could no longer bear to watch my people suffer. I fight for their liberation and for the freedom of every life on Earth.

I hope and pray for peace and happiness for all southerners, and for all the people of Thailand.

Foreward II

    I had the opportunity to read an article written by Dr.Sompong Dumdeang that you have kindly sent me to read. As a local citizen in the province of Pattani, I have been talking about the politically turbulent problems of the three border provinces of Thailand. I have read articles and the contents of those articles from some other journals, but I have not seen that point like this article. Besides that, I am from the local area of Pattni and have a feeling of being in harmony with the Islamic Community, which in the past period has not been discussed as much as in the present day in the three border southern provinces of Thailand that have inserted to create value among the Muslim community.

    The author of this article would probably have studied more deeply than I have read and have even learned. When I read, it caused me to feel that the current events are affecting me directly, that is, the lack of safety in life and property.

    The problems of unrest in three southern border provinces of Thailand is a political conflict related to the cultural dimension that must be resolved through the principles of peace solution, not the military solution that requires consciousness and reason.

    I hope peace in the three southern border provinces of Thailand will be realized in the very near future if government agencies of the state can apply the guidelines for solving the problems that the author has written and analyzed into 4 main factors be applied for.

Prompunt Kulthawee

As a native of Pattani Province and president of the Teachers

Association group of Kuankalong, Satun Province

8 May 2022, 13.51 p.m.

Foreword III

In 2003, the author brought his family, who had settled and resided in the United States, back to his hometown to visit relatives and siblings in the southern part of Thailand after the author had written for decades, having settled in America for over 50 years, the writer brought his second son with him. It turned out that Peter had dengue fever due to being bitten by a mosquito, causing severe symptoms and requiring him to be hospitalized at Phuket Provincial Hospital for 3 weeks. With the expertise of the doctor who provided care, the treatment was of an international standard comparable to World-class patient care

A team of 2-3 doctors narrowly saved the author's son, Peter, from danger.

The author would like to express his deepest gratitude to the team of doctors who treated him. All three doctors showed great respect to the author. The author would also like to thank the hospital and medical staff who Take care of and take care of your son to avoid danger as safely as possible.

Because the son of the writer Sakyan has the word "black and red" on his right shoulder, the doctor who treated Peter understood that the patient who had the word "black and red" on his shoulder was the author of the book "Dhamma that makes the mind free and free from germs" and another book called With the story of politics in the southern border provinces, under the name of Sompong Dumdeang, the writer, which the three doctors had read and liked the writing. However, those doctors did not ask who the writer was. When they saw the word Dumdeang on the son's right shoulder, they assumed it was the writer. But they always wondered how it was possible that a writer of reliable Dharma and politics would be old. Just this little one.

When the author revealed himself as the author of the two books, the author was welcomed by the doctors who treated the patients with joy and invited the author to speak on the stage in the hospital conference room on the day the author's son was to be discharged from the hospital.

On that day, a doctor stood up and said, *"Doctor, the two books you wrote are It is valuable and useful to the readers. It will be useful to the general public and it is also very useful to the southern people. Therefore, I would like to ask permission from the writer to print both books for distribution to medical personnel, patients and the general public."*

The author has given permission to publish it with full willingness and with great pleasure. It was very impressive, causing the participants in the meeting that day to applaud the author in honor. The author himself will never forget the impression of that time. In addition, the group of doctors who cured Peter from dengue fever agreed with the hospital that they would not charge a fee. The hospital's donation at that time, which was a very high amount of money, was considered a great kindness of the hospital.

The author believes in the good karma that the author gave as alms according to the teachings of the Lord Buddha, which clearly brought benefits to Peter Dumdeang. It is a pity that the authors of The manuscripts of both books were not kept. Only the photocopy was kept. It may be reprinted for the benefit of Buddhists in general. As for the book on solving the problems in the 3 southern border provinces, it will be considered again whether it should be reprinted as a book or not. This is because the writer and the other Co-authored and currently publishing the book "Crisis of Conflict in the 3 Southern Border Provinces."

The book on solving the problems of the three southern border provinces that the author had written and was banned by the government at that time from being published was a revelation of horror. It was also a great challenge for the author as a writer because the author's brother was brutally murdered, which was a cruel killing. You and the Wild Forest At last, Phiphat Dumdeang, the author's elder brother, was a senior civil servant teacher. Nowadays, he would be called a director or a high-level administrator in Pattani Province.

The loss of his elder brother and assistant in the incident that occurred more than 40 years ago was a great loss for the Dumdeang family. No words can describe the sorrow at that time.

The author had the opportunity to work with General San Chitpatima, former Deputy Commander-in-Chief of the Royal Thai Army, and Chief of Staff Sura Sak Son Suea, District Chief of Nong Chik, and other relevant officials at that time, who provided great cooperation and assistance. The author spent his life on the battlefield with military and police officers and other civilians. He slept where he slept at night, along with other officials. Relentlessly, in order to track down the perpetrator who killed the author's brother, he even went into the tunnel in the 19th building to gather information about the perpetrator and to follow up on the opposing side's operational plan.

Both General San Chitpatima and Colonel Surasak Sonsue went to appear there and praised Phi Phiphat Dumdeang, who said that he truly loved the writer's brother. The writer studied ROCT (Reserved Officer Corps Training) at Washington University, which is a program for those who will graduate with a doctorate degree. Everyone must pass this course, and the results of this study helped the writer to apply it in the investigation to find the killer who killed the writer's brother very well.

The governor of Songkhla Province at that time gave great cooperation to the writer. He told the write: *"I would like to inform you, Doctor, that I feel as sorry and sad as the Dumdeang family who have lost Khru Phiphat Dumdeang. He was a sincere person who honestly helped the government in the work he was responsible for. He was honest to his commanders, children, people, and promises. He promised me everything, I remember. I trusted him a lot. He kept his word and succeeded in everything. He should be a military or police officer rather than a civil servant."*

General San Jitpatima said in a trembling voice on the day of the author's brother's funeral that.

"I love Teacher Piwat like one of my own brothers."

The author wrote to General San that he would like to thank him very much for showing his love to his brother and his family. My brother is a lucky person who had the opportunity to work with him and serve the country together. General San went on to say that.

"Another thing is that we are proud of Khru Pipat who has done only good deeds, served the country with honesty and with great sacrifice for the peace of the people in the South and all Thai people in the country. Even though he is gone, he has left behind good things, and his good deeds will definitely lead him to a good place."

In addition, General San also invited the writer to join hands to help the country because it is time for someone with knowledge and ability, like the doctor, to join hands to continue the work of his brother for the benefit and happiness of the people of the South and all Thai people.

"Doctor, this is my request so that you can review and take the time to work together to serve the nation."

The author expressed his deepest gratitude and vowed to work for the country as requested by trying to push this piece of writing to completion as soon as possible.

Out of concern for the safety of the Dumdeang family, the provincial governor at that time issued an order to evacuate the Dumdeang family from the dangerous area. The author himself had the opportunity to consult with the former Minister of the Interior, Mr. Samak Sunthorawet, to request an increase in the police force to patrol and ensure the safety of all the author's relatives and siblings and to set up a police station. The Khuan Kalong police arrived quickly, and he quickly handled it.

The author is deeply grateful for the kindness of Her Royal Highness Princess Maha Chakri Sirindhorn, whose thoughts are reflected in the book Southern Culture, which is beneficial to the author and readers. For the reasons stated, both authors have the same opinion and named this book **"Crisis of Political and Religious Conflict in the 3 Southern Provinces of Thailand"**.

With best wishes from the author.

Dr. Sompong Dumdeang

Table of Contents

Chapter 1: Introduction	1
Chapter 2: Fire spreads under the sea	8
Chapter 3: What is terrorism?	13
Chapter 4: Crisis...Conflict 3 Southern Border Provinces	20
Chapter 5: The government is urgently trying to extinguish the smoke from the southern fires. To bring it to a close as soon as possible.	33
Chapter 6: Put out the fire under the fire	51
Chapter 7: Let's review and talk about the problem The unrest in the South	57
Chapter 8: Vicious Cycle In the 3 Southern Border Provinces	65
Chapter 9: Closing remarks	82
Chapter 10: Summary and Suggestions for Solving the Problem: The unrest in the three southern border provinces	88
Conclusions and recommendations for resolving the conflict in the three southern border provinces of Thailand	94
Bibliography	105

1
Introduction

Thailand is a land that foreigners admire as beautiful, and foreigners from all over the world have come to travel to admire the beauty of our land for a long time. However, as a country in Asia that has beautiful tourist spots that are very attractive to tourists, Thailand still has its own internal problems. That is the problem of conflict in the southern border provinces of Thailand. The problem of terrorism that occurred in the South has been widely discussed and debated as a problem that Thai people have faced since the past until today. What the terrorists in the South of Thailand have done is an attempt by They are trying to tear Thailand into two parts by the separatist movement that uses violence as a bargaining power to. The objective is to let society see the roots of the conflict and what is happening.

At present, it may be a big goal to have a bargaining power in negotiating with the government as well.

This has led to a rift between Thai Buddhists and Thai Muslims. The Thai government has also made grave mistakes in its approach to solving the problem. The conflict in Thailand's southern border provinces is a delicate issue that has been widely discussed and analyzed. Both authors jointly analyzed that the problem that has occurred is a problem that It is mainly caused by violent Muslims, which occur in some of the most critical areas in the world. Since the author began writing this book in 2004, no less than 2,000 children have been lost, and thousands more adults have fallen victim to the brutality of violence.

Both authors have detailed the problems that have occurred since 2004, using information from many sources. They found that fifty percent of those killed or murdered were Muslims themselves, and the killers or murderers were Muslims who worked for the Thai government.

Or, if it were otherwise, it could be considered an act of defying Allah. For example, at first, Muslims were not allowed to work on Fridays because working on Fridays would be considered a violation of the commandments of Allah.

The targets of the violent Muslim groups have gradually expanded, with the initial targets being soldiers, and only police officers were included. Later, it was expanded to include other types of civil servants, including village headmen, doctors, nurses, and even court justice officers. Teachers are another important target for terrorist groups, as teachers are close to the people and act as a representatives of the state.

The radicals want to steal the masses from the government. Threatening and threatening teachers to create fear, such as what happened to the author's brother. The assassination unit followed the author's brother all the time. When they met Opportunity to commit brutal killings. The result of this violence is that the Thai population in the 3 southern border provinces is the largest proportion of the population without education, the highest among all regions of Thailand.

Islam, the dream of Muslims

Living together, living as brothers and sisters in the same world, all of them are brothers and sisters because everyone lives in the world together. "Islam is a worldly matter, it is universal, it is a far-sighted religion. Therefore, eliminating religion will make it a narrow matter. Do not reduce the height of Islam, but do not take the worldview that is Narrow to the point of self-isolation. Islam is a religion that is related to all human beings.

The problem of violence of terrorism, which has caused unrest in the 3 southern border provinces, is a problem for all Thai people. As stated in the royal speech of Her Majesty the Queen, "People in religion must be full of compassion. Islam is a religion that creates people to Be humble to everyone. Therefore, Islam condemns the use of violence to cause violence both in Thailand and abroad. It condemns the use of violence to solve various problems, including human rights. More than this, They believe that if anyone believes in any religion, they will reach peace when they reach this noble truth. Allah desires peace."

What situations is the government concerned about? The situation of demanding the rights of the people in this area of the country in the form of democracy may escalate beyond its capacity. This problem has The details and depth of the problem itself are worth studying and analyzing deeply to the core. Know the truth, and then you can solve the next problem. The problem is serious and severe. Let everyone think of the kindness of the land. May the whole nation help to think of solutions to the southern problems with the great power of both of their kings who have made the daily killings cease. May the divine guardian of Siam protect and solve the southern problems with compassion and unity, with clear understanding and true understanding, and develop and integrate to suppress the southern fires forever and continuously.

When it comes to stability in the eyes of Thai Muslim brothers and sisters in the 3 southern border provinces, where the majority of the population is Muslim, approximately 80 percent, and the minority of the population is Buddhist, only about 15 percent. However, the majority of the people of the nation, all 77 provinces, have also been following the situation. Along with anxiety, especially The period after Thaksin Shinawatra's government began to administer as the Prime Minister of Thailand in 2001, there was no peace in the country. Instead of loud music, we heard the sound of guns and bombs all around the platform of Hat Yai Railway Station, Songkhla Province, which Ng is the birthplace of the author.

On April 7, 2001, there were several bombings in the southern border provinces. There was an attempt to shoot an officer who was arresting someone for ransom almost. It can be called a "daily tradition," including the brutal beheading of two people. This was something that happened during Thaksin Chinnawat's time. From that time until This time, things are not getting any better because of the killings, bombings, and destruction of life and property is still happening continuously without stopping.

For example, when Thai Buddhists issued a special statement 1/2558 during the government of General Prayut Chan-o-cha, condemning the killing of Buddhist religious leaders, the monks' safety protection team, and the Buddhist volunteer network. Yala Province announced the "incident Regarding the unrest in Sai Buri District, Pattani Province." At the same time, many organizations have come out to express their regret and condemn the actions of the terrorist movement of the southern bandits but do not believe that the media is affiliated with the southern bandit movement will come out to respond that "only one monk died "The whole country is in a state of drama." During the month of Ramadan, armed groups of people caused incidents. They bombed local leaders, Islamic religious leaders, and Thai Muslims who were traveling to pray at the mosque, but there was no mention of it.

Why does society not see the importance? Because the people who believed the propaganda of the past movements began to see the true nature of Satan that lurks in people's bodies. Because every action is the answer. No one needs to point the finger and accuse the movements of being bad... In a short while, these evil organizations will collapse. At that time, the people of Pattani will be able to sleep without having bad dreams anymore... Peace and happiness that everyone Everyone is waiting for it to arrive.

However, we must admit frankly that the government in the era of Thaksin Shinawatra is a "lost" government or in the English language, it is called a "mishand" by assessing the situation as the action of a "petty thief" and also asking the journalists to help spread false news that was not true to the event that "everything, the state is on the right track." The word that the state is on the right track and the state at present is still not enough "good but not good enough" is good for the state but not enough for the villagers of the 3 southern border provinces of ours. Duties must be performed to protect the lives and security of our Thai brothers and sisters, both Thai Muslims and Thai Buddhists, to a greater extent. Because it is still clear that daily killings are occurring, how can one speak wholeheartedly that the state is on the right track? Delegating power and domestic security policies to the Minister of the Interior The National Police Commander, The Commander of Provincial Police Region 9, is responsible for transferring the Border Patrol Police that used to be under tactical control from the Supreme Military Command back to the normal command level. There is an order to return soldiers on duty in the field to the normal divisions.

The author would like the readers to ask the question, "Who ordered it? Because the results of the action did not benefit all the southern brothers and sisters. Since that day, the terrorist movement in the area has only increased." Freedom of action in the city, where youths are trained to become a force, has gradually sacrificed more lives. Plus, the government officials used the "killing" system. Therefore, the situation was so bad that there were reports that we had to **"blind the enemy"** in order to win the strategy.

Looking at the opposite side to the situation of the insurgency, because the current violence is in the form of "blind the government," the work in the areas of administration, war, mass psychology and development has not been successful since the policy has been pushed because of the personal interests of the government leaders but did not consider the interests and happiness of the Thai brothers and sisters, both Thai Muslims and Thai Buddhists in the 3 southern border provinces at all.

Economic side

To be the leading direct sales, economics must invest in resources and budgets of billions of baht or more and arrange a workforce of no less than 12,000 people to win and build the "faith" of the grassroots people to achieve results quickly. We must rethink that the future plan goes wrong and fix it there. Part of the point is The dangers for the "grassroots" people are not solved.

That is, the non-commissioned officers who are in the service and have retired and who live in the villages have been in the service for a long time and have been able to build connections with influential people. These are the gangsters, the thugs in the form of the dark power gangsters who have received the dark power through their family connections from their fathers, their children and grandchildren continue the family line because they are considered. They have been the dark power for a long time. Everything they have done has become natural, normal.

These non-commissioned officers will go and establish relationships with the dark-powered thugs and do something improper, then pressure the leaders in order to cover up the problem and prevent the bad stories from reaching the commanders. If the commanders find out, it is too late to fix it. The commanders will try to survive by "covering up the problems" that have occurred, including crime and drugs, gambling, and drug trafficking. The commander is thus in a state of suffocation until the villagers do not know who to turn to for help. In the end, they have to rely on the gangsters, the dark power. It is the best opportunity for the dark power to train the villagers to be sympathetic to them and oppose the state, including the terrorist groups that It is happening today.

In the beginning, both writers emphasized the important factors in solving the problem of unrest in the 3 southern border provinces. Historical perspective, religious perspective, Malay perspective. Next, we will talk about the principles of stability strategic perspective. This is no less important than the current factors or other factors because it is related to the integration of the economy, daily life, and the struggle of local people to find money and work in the country and abroad, such as in Malaysia. Because there are 2 nationalities in many percentages, starting with what? How?

Starting with the (problem), the (solution), the (approach), the (clusters), the (command and control), and the comparison of the first and the new strategies as experienced by the author, both from observing the events that occurred and from the details of the research analysis for a long time, both in the university and from (personal views).

When we talk about strategy, we don't talk about it indiscriminately. We talk about a new strategy. The writer would like to propose to the government that under the government's urgent policy, it has created a new driving force to turn around the economy and solve the problems of the southern society of the country. However, the economic recovery and the solution to the problems of the southern society of the country have had very little impact on the development of the 3 southern border provinces.

It can be said that the driving forces of economic and social development may not yet be used as an important mechanism to seriously solve problems in the area. This is because the old problem-solving vision still uses and uses the old practices without considering the situation and the surrounding environment that has changed according to the new world that has been. It is called the "21st century".

The strategy of the 3 southern border provinces may be called the strategy "Southern Peace," meaning to make the 3 southern border provinces have peace and prosperity. Or it can be called the "2P strategy", which is creating peace and prosperity.

Therefore, the approach to solving problems in the 3 southern border provinces, the concept and the way of looking at the problem must start from looking at the problem in a "vibe" way, which is that the government must take into account the environment that is currently occurring or is occurring. The current event existing and the identity of the important area and the operation in the form of "integration" is the big point and the most important mechanism.

The policy of using politics to lead the military

When considering the policy of using politics to lead the military peacefully, It is a fundamentally correct practice, but politics must be separated because The political system by politicians is not yet democratic. Therefore, it is necessary to use Government policies as a part of leading politics to achieve results before negative results by making Terrorism problems end quickly.

Then consider the use of political policies and including nationality gently, meticulously, and deeply into the people's real feelings (grassroots) as the next step; what do they want, and where are they dissatisfied? The government must fix that point, for example, such as they do not like or are dissatisfied with the development. A leader in the materialistic world Western style but likes and wants the harmonious development of Islam It is an important example that the state must pay special attention to.

The two authors wrote this book to delve deeper into what the author had discussed with General San Jitpatima regarding the safety and security of our southern brothers and sisters. During the conversation, it was In the form of interviews and general discussions, and of course, this is the content of our book.

The author will compile personal experiences plus the experiences of Dr. Chompoo Nuchitpatima's father while he held an important military position in this book. Therefore, our content will focus on the complex political situation. During the government of Thaksin Shinawatra until the current government, will show the manual for working for the people regarding the problem of conflict in the southern border provinces of King Rama VI to find ways to help the southern people who live far away from the land that lives "with fear" to receive protection. And also pointed out the issue that the Thai government has sent troops into the area to suppress if the suppression operation is unsuccessful. Is the Thai government ready to change the way it deals with the southern border crisis? Is the Thai government ready "to use the utmost caution in solving the problem"?

The two authors will analyze the "crisis" of violence that has occurred since the beginning of 2004 and will advise the government on how to stop the "violence" of the southern insurgency, and of course, the initial approach of Dr. Chompoo Nuchitpatima's father to protect and create peace in the South.

We will point out why the author's brother, Khun Pipat Dumdeang, was killed while Dr. Chompoonuch's father, General San Chitpatima and Sergeant Surasak Sonsue were still in their positions. This book will end with A manual for civil servants in the South that His Majesty King Rama VI granted.

The two writers started writing this book about 7 years ago but had to stop because the co-writer had to be hospitalized for a long time. However, the main writer never gave up and tried to push the book out to the Book Market as soon as possible.

The author agrees with the American historian Samuel Huntington, who answered the question, If so, what causes the post-Cold War wars? He proposed a cultural hypothesis and saw that civilizational conflicts would be the cause of a future world war after the Cold War ended. The author would like to suggest to the readers that For those interested in Samuel Huntington's theory, a detailed study can be found in the book "**The Clash of Civilizations: Foreign Affairs, 1993**", which the author used as a guideline in teaching students at Washington University about the story of "Culture refers to political scholars in the field of comparative politics."

(political comparative)

The author attempts to explain democracy from the dimension of the political culture of the state using religion as the main principle and explaining to the students that in the dimension of political culture, which is considered as a daily life that is believed in, we set up a cultural issue, which indicates that the modern world today has moved away from the "ideological war" of the Cold War era. Enter the post-Cold War "Civilization War."

Therefore, the end of the Cold War, or in other words, the Cold War, has evolved into a form of liberalism, which we accept as manifested in the form of political democracy. Even political parties in some countries have named the Liberal Party as the electoral system and economic liberalism, with the marketing industry group as the representative of both of the above. It has become an important force of globalization. Globalization has driven (movement) or global trends and has driven the whole world, including the southern part of Thailand.

The South is waking up to fight for their lives in terms of economics. Liberalism is equal to Bangkok and the world. This is a global trend. The global trend is the power of globalization that has intervened in southern Thailand. The global trend has made this phenomenon a reflection of "Liberalism," which is based on a universal human ideology. It seems that there is no ideology that has enough power to challenge liberalism, such as communism in China, Russia, Kyiv, Pulo liberalism in our South, etc.

When discussing the phenomenon of the Cold War era as a world under the ideology and concept of liberalism in politics and economics, let's look at another side of the world that the author has mentioned, which is "culture," not another world. One side of the world that is under the influence of Islamic civilization has ideology and concepts that are different from Western liberalism: The end of Islamic civilization is determined by moral requirements.

Thus, the political, economic and social explanations of one's own Islam and religious teachings are considered universal to the Muslim world, unlike the liberal world, which is considered universal to the Western world.

In short, stories like this reflect political change where the ideological war has ended, but the civilization war is beginning. There is a question of whether the civilization war should have a compromise for peace rather than a war-like killing, and this is the creation of stability and the solution to the southern insurgency problem.

"We both have to admit that it's not easy, General (General San)," the writer replied.

"The southern region had a lot of southern fires before, but it didn't spread and spread like it does now, such as during the Communist Party era, the separatist movement. But the war can end the southern problem and make it less severe as if there was nothing." (Referring to the conversation between General San Chitpatima and the writer, Dr. Sompong Dumdeang, on January 30, 2519)

All of the above, including the new episodes for acceptance For change, don't drink the new system, just the newness, the new person is a good person with a new perspective, a new worldview, new knowledge, new understanding, a new organization (to join the new person, such as the new person, the most prepared strategy) The most New management It must be directly involved in fostering a "new culture." How can Islam/Buddhism be integrated into the social sector, which is called dialogue or reconciliation?

When there was a funeral for my brother, sister, father, and mother, more than 50 Muslim brothers and sisters gathered at the Buddhist temple. They were dressed in Western clothes. The writer did not know that he was Muslim, so he was invited to come up and offer the funeral pyre. He apologized, saying that he was Muslim and could not do it. He came because of the good deeds of the deceased. The writer was delighted and very happy because he talked and reconciled with us Thais. We should find the principles. New cultures apply examples in the southern society to achieve a new culture of problem management that must lead to ownership, unity and collective action.

This is another attempt to present a solution to the problems in the southern border provinces that is not just a matter of the cause and the issue but a matter of dialogue and reconciliation, as the author has suggested at the beginning, which is directly related to the creation of new people, new organizational strategies and new management.

The hope is for the state mechanism directly to be able to create strength for the efficiency in solving the southern problems in the future, and the southern people will have a future that is happy, cool and has a sense of stability and security in their own lives for their children and grandchildren to continue on in other areas in Thailand. If the reader follows up and reads this book to the end, you can predict what will happen to our future.

2
Fire spreads under the sea

For many years, the author has been interested and has spent time researching and following up on the stories of unrest in the 3 southern border provinces of Thailand, the conflicts between races and conflicts between religions, languages, ideologies, and cultures throughout daily life, terrorism in the South, terrorism of Muslims, and violations of human rights, which have become the history of our Thai nation. Rooted in the rule of the Hindu-Buddhist kings who controlled the sea from the peninsula to the Gulf of Bengal.

Let's take the readers to study the historical dimensions of the land of civilization that used to flourish to the fullest in the most magnificent way in the past. It was very important until the present day. Pattani, Yala, and Narathiwat provinces, which appear on the map of Today's Thailand, a land that has hidden many things from the past, including history, customs, traditions, politics, linguistics, and other things that are so complicated that it is difficult for us, the younger generation, to understand them in detail, except for those who are particularly interested in this area of the country.

From the study and research, it was found that this land was once the land of the Hindu-Buddhist or Hindu-Java or Hindu-Islamic Kingdom, which received the civilization flowing from the Gulf of Bengal. In addition, it was mixed with the Chinese civilization in the east. At that time, Pattani was called "Lankasuka," which was the name of the city (i) Lankasoka, which is Sanskrit, namely Sangka-Ashoka, which means "The Union City of Asoke" (which is called Pattani-Darusalam Rattiya Sale in "Srivichai" page 239) appears as a name according to the records of Chinese travelers who came to trade with various countries in Southeast Asia around the 2nd century. Lang-Ya Shiu or Lankasu It already existed, but no one could confirm who founded the Kingdom of Lankasuka and the Kingdom of Pattani. Therefore, it is believed that the Kingdom of Lankasuka controlled trade from the peninsula to the Gulf of Bengal. Later, the name "Pattani" appeared in the 13th century.

Pattani

The country is a big family. If you try to understand your children well, which is called understanding them and understanding yourself, the family will be peaceful and happy when the Thai government comes to make things happy. Setting assumptions that you know them and you know us to make it possible and being able to follow up on and solve crises in the 3 southern border provinces to keep up with the real events is still a complicated and long-lasting matter. In our Thai history, the lack of true and clear unity still arises from the fact that the rulers of the country have not yet surrendered their power or agreed to decisively surrender their administrative power (sound decision), resulting in unity of command (unity of company). In layman's terms, it is still not a true single command, such as giving absolute command of authority to the 4th Army as the leader in the modern era. Under the Cool Shade, all units have agreed to comply with the principles and conditions of the "Under the Cool Shade" policy, etc.

But when it comes to the government of Thaksin Shinawatra, it may fall into the trap of missing the schedule. The strategy to stop the southern fire has been wrong since the beginning of the administration of the country. The news media is dark with the phrase "petty thieves," so the killings have happened. There is a huge budget that is quite excessive.

The author would like to present a geographical dimension to pave the way for understanding.

The southern part of Thailand is an axe-shaped area, which is called the "axe" extending down to the equator in the south, known as the "Malay Peninsula," dividing the sea into two parts: the west is adjacent to the Indian Ocean, the east is adjacent to the Gulf of Thailand, and the present Pacific Ocean.

The southern part of Thailand is rich in forests. The area is densely forested, with both rice fields and fisheries and a variety of other occupations. There are many ways for people in this region of Thailand to make a living. Whoever owns this "territorial strategy" area may become a millionaire with sufficient resources as desired and can control the trade routes from the east to the west through the Kra Isthmus and also have power.

Both of them are concerned with human rights, especially women and children, both in Thailand and around the world and in the three southern border provinces of Thailand. If we take the definition of international human rights law, it has been determined that the state must protect innocent citizens, including children and women.

Even in times of war, there are important regulations to protect women who are pregnant and mothers of young children. They prohibit the destruction of women's dignity, such as rape, forced prostitution, and harm to women, including the control of women and the execution of women.

However, in our three southern border provinces at present, It is almost impossible to say that violations of human rights are occurring almost every day. For example, on July 9, 2014, a female nursing student intern at a local hospital in Yala Province was brazenly shot with a gun by a number of assailants in full view of the public.

Such actions greatly terrify and horrify the local people, making them feel increasingly insecure about their lives in this region. It also reflects the brutality of life, the easy way to see the lives of the opposing side as worthless, which is something that has occurred due to the conflict situation in the southern border region. The wide range of such incidents has been repeated, raising the question of why both sides do not hope for a peaceful resolution instead of considering the role and future of the civil society that can solve our problems, including unity in solving them.

Thai lessons

Unity in solving the problem to use Thai security to have the same direction as the West, as we can clearly see. That is, the perspective that views the threat has become a factor or factor that has a direct role in linking the policy of "Thai security" to become a part of the movement in itself of the "globalization trend" in terms of the security of our brothers, the United States.

The important result of looking at the problem in this way is to see that the wars that have occurred in the areas around Thailand are the result of the support of the Communist Party from outside, and the more the US leaders present the idea of the "domino theory" of the US falling in the region, which means the phenomenon that if any state in this area falls, it will fall under the domination of the Communist Party and the aforementioned bankruptcy will occur to the neighboring states. The method used is to create a war of insurgency within those states.

Therefore, the strategic concerns for Thai leaders have always existed because of this characteristic. According to the dictionary and the explanation of the Domino Theory it clearly shows that if Indochinese countries have to become socialist states, it is difficult to escape.

In the past few years, Thaksin has tried every means to change the system of government to be a socialist state as desired, relying on the reason of the leader. Some Thais still believe in democracy and disagree with Thaksin's political party. Thailand has thus narrowly escaped the threat of the Red Shirts. However, the stability of democracy remains in a dangerous position.

Thus, such concerns may be explained by either the (socialization) in the learning process of the Thai leaders from the West, led by the United States at present, or it may be due to the ongoing fears of the Thai elite since the changes of government in China and Russia.

As a result of such resolutions, the Thai elite at that time turned to establishing an official alliance with the United States as a tool to reduce the aforementioned concerns. For example, Thanat-Rust's accession to the Southeast Asian Organization (SEATO) in 1955 became an important "symbol" of Thailand's foreign policy and security. It indicates the main direction in the strategy of fighting the communist war.

In such a situation, it seems that Thai leaders are more interested in the external conditions of war than the internal ones. In particular, Thai military leaders tend to believe that if war causes unrest in Thailand, it will be based on external support. Thai soldiers will not put too much weight on internal conditions.

If asked why... it is because the Communist Party of Thailand is seen as just a "branch" of the Chinese Communists. In addition, it is also believed that the conditions of the Thai people themselves to take up arms to fight (armed insurgency) against the state should not be impossible, whether explained by the conditions of the Thai people or the characteristics of Thai Buddhist society.

The fact that they devoted their strength to both military and financial aspects, interested in preventing the Thai Communist Party's war from occurring only because of external support, in order to prevent the Communist Party from expanding and infiltrating external communists, the theory of the Thai military and government leaders, which the author has learned, can be summarized simply that the Thai Communist

War will occur, only with external support. When this is the case, Thailand should devote its strength and resources to prevent the expansion of communism from outside.

If the reader looks back at the history of the unrest caused by the Communist Party, do not forget that the members of the Thai Communist Party are not "strangers" in our Thai society which is a Communist Party they are leaders of students, political activists, leaders of workers, leaders of farmers, etc. This war is clearly an internal war, but at the same time, it does not mean that it has any relationship with external factors to the problem of "internal stability."

Therefore, the author would like to repeat the Thai leader's principle that with the mentioned political situation, it seems that the Thai leader has turned to be interested in the conditions of the war. From the cause or external factors (the world), knowing only the Thai military leader who firmly believes that if the war causes unrest in Thailand, it is because of external support.

For this reason, the author's Military leadership does not place much weight on internal conditions. The Communists, the Communist Party of Thailand, are seen as just a "branch" of the Chinese Communists. This is unlikely to be an explanation, whether it is based on the Thai personality or the characteristics of Thai Buddhist society.

In the author's opinion, when mentioning such a view, to summarize simply, the reader should understand that the communist war or the Thai communist party war can only occur with external support. When this happens, the Thai state should devote all its forces and resources to prevent the expansion of communism from outside.

The author believes that they will forget that in the globalization Evolution of the Cold War Era, There was a flow of ideas like Thai leaders (former students abroad, Especially from the United States, etc. who had gone through the learning process from the Western camp. But another group of people had different ideas from the state. They may have gone through the learning process from the Western camp, which is in the globalization process, the political process occurred. From being both knowledgeable and transferring political ideas to people in the group of ideas, the integrated political system cannot be distinguished from both sides.

In the writer's opinion, although the personnel of the Thai Communist Party at that time were close to the Chinese Communist Party, we must not forget that the communist war in Thailand was entirely a matter of external factors. (It is impossible for politics, culture, etc.; it is related to All chains being connected) and in fact, the dialogue of the members of the Thai Communist Party in various eras has also been a conflict of ideas that makes the war depend on our own internal conditions in Thailand, which makes the war depend on repeated internal conditions only more than making the people's war in Thailand.

Let's look back at the Thai Communist Party's insurgency war, which started in 1965 and continued until 1982/1983 when the Thai government declared victory in the war.

Strategically (History) of the government's warfare can be roughly divided into two periods, which the author sees as the first period from 1963-1980 (15 years) in which military operations were fully used to respond to the expansion of the communist party (some of the theories have been put into practice in the new form of BRN in Pattani today) especially after 1967, the dedication of military forces in The countryside has become the main approach as well as the operation of sending soldiers to suppress the conflict in the South. Currently, the military is the main method for solving the problems in the South. And this approach also sees communism as an "alien" to Thai society and Thai politics.

Therefore, there are no Thais who are communists. Only foreigners are communists or groups of people who have been brainwashed by foreigners, which makes the use of force to suppress them right and just in itself because of the belief of the Thai military government that these people are not Thais or are a group of people who have been brainwashed to the point of not being Thais, because in the concept or in the definition itself, Thais are not communists.

The author, therefore, believes that the conflict between the Chinese and Vietnamese Communist parties over the invasion of Cambodia in 1979 has become an opportunity to open up the relationship and stability between the Thai-Chinese governments and tighten The result was that the Thai Communist Party quickly faced the unpredictable situation of the impact of the aforementioned tightening of relations, which led to a reduction in the party's military operations, leading to a state of retreat, and finally the People's War in Thailand officially ended in 1982-1983.

3
What is terrorism?

Terrorism is one of the forms of warfare in history. However, the form of terrorist warfare is different from the forms of warfare commonly known as total warfare, limited warfare, general warfare, guerrilla warfare, or war of liberation. Or revolutionary war (revolution warfare).

In order to understand the meaning of the types of war in various forms, The author would like to explain the meaning of war terrorism in brief Because each form has different uses of force, tactics and objectives.

Total warfare

War or any form of warfare, not just military forces. The targets of the attack are all kinds of targets, military targets, civilian targets, and various institutions. The desired outcome is all forms: destroying the adversary, destroying the institution, and changing beliefs.

Limited warfare

It is a war that has a limited goal to destroy an area within a certain range. Such as limiting the equipment of the other side that is expected to be a danger to itself Or limiting the method of fighting by not using certain weapons to prevent the war from spreading, Such as not using aircraft or nuclear weapons.

General warfare

Sometimes called a conventional war, it is a war that uses forces from the army, navy, and air force, which are forces that are organized according to the military.

Guerilla warfare

It is a war that has a rather special characteristic. Namely, it is conducted with a small force. It uses a small amount of weapons but has a broad target, using disturbance or using time as a tool to delay the adversary from advancing in the operation.

There are now many different movements opposing their governments in many countries. These movements have similar aims of demanding freedom and autonomy or liberation from government control. These movements may stem from ethnic or religious beliefs.

It is considered or may be derived from the promotion or support of any country for political or other benefits of the country that provides such support, even the promotion or support of mutual assistance during the process.

War of Terrorism

The terrorists do not have military uniforms, even though their fighting methods are military-like, and their weapons do not necessarily have to be military-style weapons. No one can tell who the terrorists are because they are dressed like ordinary civilians. The weapons they use can be anything that can cause panic or fear among the people. To be used as a tool to press or negotiate what he wants.

Conventional war

It is a war that has rules of battle on the battlefield, rules and regulations stipulated by law, especially international law, treatment of civilians and prisoners of war who are captured both during the war and or after the war has ended, and most importantly, it is a battle between soldiers and soldiers in uniform on both sides.

Terrorists

Use of terrorism in various forms as weapons, which do not have to be guns or bombs alone like soldiers in the general army. The target of terrorism depends on the time and place, or it may be a house or in a community, even on an airplane, on a commercial ship, at a port, or at an airport.

Assassination

The hijacking of individuals or vehicles, burning, causing panic, or planting bombs in various places are important weapons of terrorism that require little manpower and cost, but the impact is vast and incalculable.

There are more than ten armed forces in the southern region. Some are politically motivated, some are conventionally armed, and some do both. They are divided into three groups:

- One group has only political goals.
- Group 2 has only armed forces that commit crimes.
- The three groups are armed forces that operate both politically and criminally.

However, according to various sources, it is generally agreed that among these groups, there are Muslim separatist groups and armed communist forces, both Thai Muslim and Thai Buddhist, with the most dangerous being hired gunmen who claim to be separatist groups and hired gunmen who are hired by the group. The city is hired to carry out activities in its own name.

Who is this group?

Communists and separatists, whose common goal is to destabilize the region, have both benefited from the problems in relations between the Thai and Malaysian governments over allegations of providing shelter to terrorists in their respective border areas. However, The two sides fell out in 1981 due to a dispute over the territory of Betong District, Yala Province, which was under the control of the Communist Party of Malaysia (CPM), because the Pulo group quickly intervened, causing the Pulohan group to join hands with the Thai army.

This group is their rogue group. The author means that they demand protection money, kidnap and murder. For their goals, the separatist groups are broadly similar, but rarely do they work together.

In terms of the operators themselves, no one is as vulnerable to widespread support as Haji Sulong. In the end, attempts to join hands failed, and large groups encountered internal conflicts that led to divisions.

Therefore, the government itself, after nearly twenty years of fighting the separatist groups, including communists in the South, finally realized that fighting them would require politics as well as the military. In 1981, the government overhauled its security and administrative structures in order to shift towards a more political approach. It appears that the new approach to public participation has reduced the level of violence, and hundreds of people have turned back, including communist terrorists and separatist radicals, who have come out to accept the amnesty conditions and the decision of many of them to enter the political struggle in the political system has had an impact, i.e., weakening the support for the armed struggle, but at the same time, Weakening the Armed Struggle Through Reason and Truth.

The two authors clearly show the readers that when fighting with weakened weapons, they become more violent, and some of them become more evasive instead of being eliminated. This is our weak point and weak intelligence.

There are six long-established and widely recognized terrorist groups in the South, with one more added in August 2015:

1. BRN = Barisan Revolusi National
2. PULO = Pattani United Liberation Organization
3. GMIP = Pattani Islamic Mujahideen Movement
4. BBMP = United Mujahideen Front of Pattani
5. JI = Jemaah Islamiyah
6. RKK = Runda Kumpulan Kecil
7. The new group is a combination of all the groups to form a negotiating organization with the state, calling itself Mara Pattani.

Transnational crime, terrorism

Associate Professor Dr. Panithan Wattanayagorn, Faculty of Political Science, Chulalongkorn University, former Deputy Secretary-General to the Prime Minister for Political Affairs, served at the Prime Minister's Office in the Abhisit Vejjajiva government. He is a Prime Minister as a security expert and was one of the people who participated in the drafting of the Internal Security Act of 2551 said that Thailand is currently facing two overlapping problems:

Thailand is both a base for transnational crime and a base for terrorism.

Transnational crime is a big issue that includes a variety of problems here. The National Security Council has previously issued a report on threats in a new format stating that transnational crimes include illegal immigration, money laundering, human trafficking, and drug trafficking, and one of these are international terrorist organizations included in transnational crimes.

As for international terrorism, It will be a case of international terrorist groups traveling into Thailand to use for planning, including causing unrest with the embassy, which is a target.

An interesting point is that Thailand is a base for transnational crime groups, especially arms trafficking or human trafficking, which Thai security agencies are very concerned about and have tried to solve this problem for many governments but have not been successful. Thailand is also a base for international terrorists.

The international terrorist movement that used Thailand as a base to enter and make plans is quite as clear as Malaysia, especially after the September 11 incident, which was increasingly discussed in the security forum between Thailand and Malaysia, especially during that period when the terrorists were in Malaysia.

Thailand has many problems that have the United States, Japan, Australia and Singapore worried because Thailand lacks good inspection efficiency, such as the problem of fake passports, which has led to a shocking problem of fake passports in Thailand. In the case of the police arresting a suspect who was involved in the Erawan Shrine bombing at Ratchaprasong, he was arrested at the apartment. A condo in the Min Buri district was found with a large number of passports in the rented room, and the arrested person was holding a Turkish passport but was denied by the Turkish authorities as not being Turkish. In addition, there were forged documents, ATM cards, and credit cards, all of which were involved in terrorist activities. There are more than 20 international terrorist groups operating in Thailand.

Thailand has many problems that have worried the United States, Japan, Australia and Singapore because Thailand lacks good efficiency in checking, such as the problem of fake passports, which has caused a shocking problem of fake passports in Thailand. In the case of the police arresting a suspect who was involved in the Erawan Shrine bombing at Ratchaprasong, he was arrested at an apartment in Min Buri. It was found that there were a number of passports. Many were found in the rented room, and those who were arrested held Turkish passports, but The Turkish authorities denied that he was not Turkish. In addition, there were forged documents, ATM cards, and credit cards, all of which were involved in terrorism. There are more than 20 international terrorist groups operating in Thailand.

Shockingly, Thai security agencies have admitted that Thailand has at least 20 international terrorist groups registered in the country, which the security agencies are on high alert for. The arrest of the JI leader in Ayutthaya several years ago was a major shock to the security sector.

Ridduan Isamuddin, or "Hambali," the leader of the JI terrorist group, and two of his associates were arrested by Thai authorities and the CIA, along with bombs and a computer containing information leading to the belief that he was the coordinator between Al-Qaeda and JI by setting up a tourist office. Front and back, he arranges for JI members to be sent for training and combat in troubled areas such as Afghanistan, Bosnia, Indonesia and the southern Philippines.

He often travels in and out of Malaysia, Thailand and Vietnam. Hambali sneaked into Thailand and lived in Ayutthaya province before the APEC summit, which Thailand is hosting. In October 2003, he was arrested and extradited to the United States as a fugitive, where he was tried and imprisoned in the United States.

In 2008, the Thai authorities arrested Mr. Viktor Bout, who was accused by the US of being a Russian arms dealer, while the plane stopped at Don Mueang Airport to refuel. The Thai authorities also returned Mr. Bout to the US as requested. Thailand itself must give importance to a clear position with foreign countries closely in disaster relief, coordination and the crackdown on illegal activities in Thailand. Only the fake passport process must be dealt with.

In Thai passports, there are usually gangs that steal passports to resell them and then gangs buy fake passports to resell them again. It is an illegal operation, a crime, and we do not know what the buyers are buying it for, whether it is terrorism or international crime. Either way, it is not good for Thailand.

International terrorism

The world's most influential and influential terrorist organizations Currently, there are 2 organizations: Al-Qaeda and ISIS. The author would like to understand these 2 organizations, not to admire or support their behaviors or activities, but to study and learn about the background and causes that led to the emergence of terrorist organizations that create fear around the world and have The impact on the peace of the world society is as follows: Al-Qaeda terrorist group.

It is an international terrorist group of Islamic origin, founded by Osama bin Ladin and Abdullah al-Azzam, along with several other fighters, sometime between August 1988 and late 1989, with origins dating back to the Soviet war in Afghanistan.

Al-Qaeda operates as a network consisting of a multi-national stateless army and the radical Islamic Wahhabi Jihad. The Security Council, the North Atlantic Treaty Organization, the European Union, the United States, Russia, India, and several other countries have declared the organization a terrorist organization. Al-Qaeda launched attacks on targets it considered **(kafirs)** during the Syrian civil war. Al-Qaeda separatists began fighting among themselves, the Kurds, and the Syrian government.

Al-Qaeda has carried out attacks on civilian and military targets in several countries, including the September 11, 2001 World Trade Center attacks, the 1998 U.S. Embassy bombings, and the 2002 Bali bombings. The U.S. government responded to the September 11 attacks by launching the "War on Terror" at the cost of its leaders.

The organization's key personnel, including Osama bin Ladin, The specific techniques used by Al-Qaeda include suicide attacks and simultaneous multiple target bombings. Activities attributed to Al-Qaeda may involve members of the movement who have pledged allegiance to Osama bin Ladin or large numbers of "al-Qaeda-linked" individuals who have been trained in one of the camps. In Afghanistan, Pakistan, Iraq or Sudan who did not pledge allegiance to Usama Bin Ladin

The ideology of al-Qaeda has been completely denigrated by foreign influences. Among the beliefs of the members of al-Qaeda are The ruling that the Christian-Jewish alliance is conspiring to destroy Islam because it is Salafist Jihadist and that they are indifferent to all religious texts, which may be interpreted as Killing civilians and fighting Both sides (Internecine) Al-Qaeda also strongly oppose what is called human law and wants to replace it with strict Sharia law.

Al-Qaeda is also responsible for inciting violence among Muslim sects. Its leader, Usama Bin Ladin, was killed by US naval forces in Pakistan in 2554 and was replaced by Egyptian doctor Ayman ash-Zawahiri.

The terrorist group ISIS (Islamic State of Iraq and Greater Syria) is a radical Sunni Muslim extremist group that has been described as savage and bloodthirsty to the point of sadism. Even al-Qaeda disapproves of the killing of Muslims and other minorities, including Christians and Lawyers. Syrian rebels burned down churches and mosques; Shia militias were responsible for suicide bombings and razed markets and other places, injuring and killing many civilians.

It could be said that the United States and its allies' war in Iraq in 2003 was the igniter of violence and terrorism in Iraq that later spread throughout the Middle East.

This radical Muslim group originated from the same place as al-Qaeda, which is dissatisfaction and anger over America's wars in Iraq and Afghanistan. It is led by Abu Bakr al-Baghdadi, who supported the Iraqi Jihadist war and joined the underground movement of Saddam Hussein that opposed the current Iraqi government.

ISIS may have more than 6,000 members, with about 6,000 fighting in Iraq and 3,000–5,000 fighting in Syria. This number may include up to 3,000 foreign fighters, including about 500 from the UK, France and elsewhere in Europe. ISIS also reportedly has a military reserve of more than 15,000 civilians.

For about three years, ISIS operated in Iraq and Syria, but in the last year or so, the border area between the two countries has lacked good control, which has allowed ISIS to become much stronger, covering both eastern and northern Syria and western and northern Iraq.

Some analysts see ISIS as more of a military force than a terrorist group. "It's a mobile military force that moves between Iraq and Syria," said Jessica Lewis, an ISIS expert at the (Washington Think Tank). *"They control a lot of territory. They have a shadow government in and around Baghdad. They have a clear goal of ruling the country." I don't know if they wanted to take Baghdad or destroy the structure of the Iraqi government, but either way, the outcome is the same: the downfall of Iraq."*

Lewis, a U.S. intelligence officer in Iraq and Afghanistan, described ISIS's operations as "a command system from the field to a command center, with a large budget and a large number of fighters, not just foreign fighters but also escaped prisoners."

They are highly skilled in urban guerrilla warfare, while the Iraqi army lacks that skill, say analysts studying jihadism in the Middle East.

4
Crisis...Conflict
3 Southern Border Provinces

The violence and unrest in the southern border provinces of Thailand, namely Pattani, Yala, Narathiwat and Satun, as well as the causes of unrest in several districts of Songkhla Province, have increased in intensity, and the intensity of violence has begun to escalate and become more frequent. Since the beginning of 2004, bombings and killings of government officials, including soldiers, police, teachers, and even officials in the justice process, as well as ordinary people and monks, have become a daily occurrence, with no sign of government policies to remedy and solve the problems in a concrete way, in order to bring peace and happiness back to our brothers and sisters. The southern border

The cause of the unrest has been pointed at the violent Muslims in the Islamic religion who are dissatisfied with the implementation of the government's policies. In particular, the violence began to develop and continued in 2004. It is linked to the wrong policies of the government at that time that rushed to send soldiers to fight in Iraq.

However, it would be wrong to focus the violence on the Muslim group alone. It would be unfair to look at only one side of the issue as a result of the seminar on human rights violations and the role of religion in reconciliation by the Multicultural Foundation in Pattani Province in March and at King Mongkut's University of Technology Thonburi. On March 11, 2008, there were many major problems related to the unrest in the 5 southern border provinces. The main issues are as follows:

1. Is the violence and unrest in the 3 southern provinces caused by the Malay ethnicity of the people in the 5 provinces?

Answer: Yes, some, but not all. It is necessary to understand the roots of the people in the 3 border provinces, including Satun and some districts in Songkhla Province. The Malay people are divided into 2 groups as follows:

1. Malay ethnic

They are people who live on the Malay Peninsula, the Malay Archipelago. They have a moderate physical appearance and have the same way of life, culture or identity. They speak Malay and are mostly Muslims. Most of them live in the 3 southern border provinces, namely Pattani, Yala, and Narathiwat and 4 districts of Songkhla Province, namely Thepa, Sabai Yoi, Chana, and Nathawi, have about 1.5 million people.

2. Malay descendant

Malays are a group of people who used to live together in the Malay Peninsula, the Malay Islands and the Pacific. They used to have the same way of life, culture or identity, religious beliefs and language as the political peoples who were the result of war, immigration or were molded. (assimilation) or marriage or from the influence of other nations that are superior to the original Malay race, such as cultural changes, language, religion, etc. Malay race, but due to reasons

These groups are found in the southern provinces of Thailand, from Chumphon, Surat Thani, Nakhon Si Thammarat, Phatthalung, Songkhla, Ranong, Phang Nga, Phuket, Krabi, Trang, Satun, including the Indian Ocean islanders such as the Orang Laut and the Moken, which have a total population of 754,672 people (according to the Statistical Office in 1990), as well as in the Bangkok Metropolitan Region, such as Samut Prakan, Nakhon Nayok, Chachoengsao, and others, totaling approximately 3.5 million people.

If we say that the conflict originated from the people in the 3 southern provinces and the 4 districts of Songkhla Province, it would not be wrong. But in reality, it originated from the sense of the ethnic group that is a minority that the Thai state is about to swallow up. Their assimilation Like the assimilation of the Mon, Lanna, Khmer, Lao and others, they are strong in maintaining their Malay identity, which is against the policy of the Thai state, which is a single, centralized state and considers Thailand as the home of the Tai people (including the Black Tai, Lue Tai, etc.) may not including the Malays.

2. Is the problem of violence caused by a distortion of Islamic principles? Because some Ustadz says that killing non-Muslims is not a sin. Is that true?

Answer: Not true. Killing people of any religion is a sin. The Islamic religion has never been distorted by scholars or religious leaders in the southern border provinces in any way. However, it may be due to the misunderstanding of some of the Ustaz who said so because they may not be true Ustaz or those who know the true religion. Or they may speak with a feeling of pressure, resentment, or because they have lost something they love, such as being discriminated against by their race. Others, who may be government officials or ordinary citizens arrested, abused, oppressed, and oppressed with injustice before, he said, with a sense of resentment and hatred. Therefore, we must know their deep history in all aspects in order to analyze the real cause of the problem so that we can find the right answer to solve the problem.

In order to analyze the causes of the unrest in the southern border provinces of Thailand and find the answers that will be the guidelines for solving the problems correctly and effectively, the author, along with Mr. Intarakiat Rod Pradit, as a co-author of this book, has been following the events and studying the root causes of the problems continuously for decades. Finally, our research team has expanded our research office by establishing It is an official research center to explore avenues of cooperation at both the domestic and international levels, with the aim of preventing conflicts worldwide. Our research team has drawn on in-depth information from research studies and seminars from local, regional, and international research centers, as well as from the U.S. Department of Defense. The author has access to political, economic, social and other information over a period of more than 30 years. The views expressed in this book are the personal views of our research team. The authors of this book, including co-authors, have no official ties to the US government in any way.

Current researchers have admitted that the chaos that has occurred around the world has become an act of revenge and a creation of disorder. The conflict has become a dragging conflict that has led to the loss of life for ordinary people, soldiers, police and government officials as a result of unresolved conflicts. The co-authors of this book told the author that the conflicts that have occurred in the southern border provinces have been occurring continuously for hundreds of years and that this problem has never been seriously resolved by past administrators. It still exists and would continue to exist if the government sector did not take serious and tangible action to resolve the problem.

For the above reasons, the writer has dedicated his life to finding a way to jointly solve the problem and is always ready to offer himself as a part of solving the problem both in the political and economic sectors of our country and for the peace of the world society and is always ready to face such a violent situation.

And in order to fulfill the royal initiative of King Rama VI who stated that *"The problems in the southern part of Siam seem to have existed for a long time and have existed in every era until the present day Thailand, the problems still exist. It is like a volcano that is ready to erupt at the right opportunity. Perhaps it is time for us to solve this long-standing problem."* By learning the past that reflects the present and the present that will affect the future."

The author is delighted and proud that Mr. Intarakiat Rodpradit, a co-author of this book, accepted the author's offer to collaborate on this manuscript without any hesitation, even though his personal life at that time was in crisis. However, due to his love for his country and his love for his fellow countrymen, his personal life problems that he had to deal with Having to take care of his wife, who had been paralyzed and unable to help herself for many years, this was not an obstacle for him to devote both time, physical and mental strength to study and analyze data, delving deeply into history to find the real root cause of the problem. He was sincere and felt extremely honored to start working with the writer without the slightest hesitation.

We both started working seriously, at least 12–14 hours a day, to get the book out to market in a timely manner. Initially, we expected to finish it in 6 months, but with the huge amount of information we received, we extended the production timeline to get it out as fast as possible. However, our writing was stalled for a long time because the co-author had to enter the After several years of treatment, it was finally completed after the co-author returned to Thailand after traveling and continuing his writing in America for 90 days at the end of 2014. We exchanged information with each other all the time.

One sentence that the co-author responded to the author via email about the information obtained from various sources is that we have received news information about the conflicts of the 3 southern border provinces. It is a huge amount of information that can be called an **(ocean of information.)**

Our team is keenly aware that most conflicts that occur within countries are acts of terrorism, which are acts of violence that cause unnecessary loss of life and economic instability. For our research team, we believe that there must be more than one side that is either opposed to or opposed to the state.

It is clear that the separatist groups must take every possible path to achieve their goal of an independent state with the right to self-governance. Mr. Intarakiat Rodpradit, a co-author of this book, has studied and observed the unrest in the southern Philippines, in the Molo Islands, where the majority of the population is Muslim, where there has been a terrorist movement to Establish as an independent Islamic state under the aegis of the movement known as the Moro Islamic Liberation Front.

This movement has been fighting the Philippine government for a long time in the form of a terrorist movement, just like other terrorist movements in other countries. There have been attempts by the Philippine government to negotiate a settlement of the conflict, but they have not been successful. In the Philippines, there is also a movement that has long been hostile to the government called the "Abu Sayyaf", which comes from a leader named Abdul Rasool Sayyaf, who is a Strong believes in the teachings of the Wahhabi sect that emphasizes the practice of using violence to protect Islam.

And the author himself has had the opportunity to travel around the world for decades. Just name a country where unrest has occurred. It can be seen that separatism is a major problem in many countries, such as the southern Philippines, Sri Lanka, Palestine and southern Thailand. Please note that when we say southern Thailand, we mean the southern part of the country. Consisting of 5 provinces: Satun, Songkhla, Pattani, Yala and Narathiwat, most of the population living in this area are Muslims.

The use of military force to carry out the sweep seems to be a daily order. Diplomatic operations are dead, or are they gone? Southern Thailand is in such a state. And the Thai government is facing serious problems in resolving the unrest that is occurring throughout the country.

The violent Muslim separatist movement began its operations in the early 1970s and gradually declined in intensity until the unrest in Thailand had almost subsided in the 1990s. However, the situation of unrest that led to violence flared up again.

Beginning in 2004, as a result of the phrase of the leader of the country at that time that the chaos and unrest that occurred, the state can control it and the state is on the right track to solve the problem. The incident that occurred was just the work of "petty thieves" because that was considered a strategy to solve the problem of the 3 southern border provinces that was completely failed by the government of Thaksin Chinnawat at that time.

And our research team would like to present an analysis of the history of this failed problem-solving as a warning to those responsible for the administration of the country and to seek cooperation with all sectors to jointly find a solution to the problem in order to bring peace back to our brothers and sisters in the southern border provinces and for the peace and happiness of our nation, which the analysts of the southern border problem have analyzed in an interesting way as follows:

The history of the problems of the 3 southern border provinces has been the center of movement in Pattani Province since the Ayutthaya era. Before this, Pattani was a city-state between the influence of Ayutthaya and the Malacca Kingdom. When the influence of Ayutthaya was strong, Pattani was also The influence of Ayutthaya or Malacca was strong. The southern cities under the rule of Thailand in the Malay Peninsula were also under Malacca, such as during the reign of King Borommatrailokanat, who sent the Ayutthaya army to attack Malacca twice but were unsuccessful. The Malacca Kingdom sent its army to attack. He took all the vassal states of Thailand, namely Pahang, Tangganu, Kalantan, and Saiburi. At the same time, the king of Malacca also performed the duty of spreading Islam.

Originally, King Indira or Sultan Ismael Shah, who was a Buddhist, had to compromise with Sultan Mansur Shah, the King of Malacca, by accepting Islam. It is said that during the time when Pattani was invaded by the Malacan army, the Buddha statues, idols and temples in Kota Mahalikhai were destroyed. Or Lankasuka or Pattani until the nature of that war is completely gone. The winner has the right to destroy symbols, symbols of power or permanent buildings that represent the identity of the enemy according to the tradition of war from the past until the present. For example, the destruction of the monument of former President Saddam, which was destroyed by the US army, or the statues of Lenin in many places in Eastern Europe were destroyed the Audition of the Soviet Union's defeat in the Cold War.

However, Pattani is still a center of prosperity because the Pattani River flows from the Gulf of Thailand to the high seas, which is well connected to the East. Therefore, its prosperity is eye-catching to many nations, especially the Western colonial nations in the 18th century after Thailand fought with Burma. In the late Ayutthaya period, between 1767 and 1786, during the reign of King Buddha Yodfa Chulalongkorn, King Chulalongkorn of Rattanakosin sent an advance army led by His Royal Highness Prince Maha Surasinghanat to attack Pattani, which was independent of Thailand because at that time Burma had influence over the Thai army. However, the Thai army defeated Sultan Ahamad.

In 1786, Thailand regained Pattani as it was before Ayutthaya was lost in 1767. When the cities of Saiburi, Trang and Kantan learned that Pattani could not resist the Thai army, they surrendered. The silver and gold trees were tributes according to the royal tradition of becoming a vassal state and he appointed Tengku Kader Kamaruddin as the lord of Pattani. However, he later betrayed the king and sent troops to attack Songkhla. After 4 days of fighting, the royal army from the capital, Songkhla army, and Nakhon Si Thammarat army were able to defeat the army of Phraya Pattani and retreat to Pattani. However, the mother army was shot and killed while sprinkling holy water at the camp gate.

The chaos in Pattani never ends. There was resistance to the Songkhla administration system, in which His Majesty King Buddha Yodfa ordered the Lord of Songkhla to be the one to control and take care of Pattani, Trang and Kantan.

Later, the British colluded with the Sultans of various cities in Malay territory with the plan at Penang, which was inherited from British officials and traders in Penang. They saw that the Thai government's occupation of the Sai Buri Canal would allow Thailand to gain power over the other states in Malay, which would obstruct the British's future interests.

The position of the governor of Pattani was chaotic and there were wars throughout the reign of King Rama I and Rama VI. The title was Phraya Chit Phakdi Sri Rattana, which was passed down. During the reign of King Chulalongkorn, he gathered the southern provinces, abolished the dependent city system, and established the southern province directly under Nakhon Si Thammarat.

At the same time, the British began to intervene directly, instigating and encouraging the lords to distance themselves from the Thai government so that they could annex the territories in the northern Malay Peninsula. In 1896, King Rama V made the southern cities come under the jurisdiction of the governor of Nakhon Si Thammarat Province, which was one way to prevent the British from easily interfering with the southern lords.

In 1901, the British in Singapore wanted to invade Thai territory on the Malay Peninsula, but the central government in London did not agree. The British in Singapore, therefore, used a trick to trick the ruler of Pattani into distancing themselves from Thailand. Phraya Pattani, or Abdul Kader, believed the British and resisted King Rama V. He was therefore arrested and detained in Phitsanulok Province. The situation was calmed down, and in 1904, Tengku Abdul Kader received the grace of King Rama V, who allowed him to return to Pattani on the condition that he would not be involved in any way with the country.

Later, when King Mongkut ascended the throne, Tengku Abdul Kader wrote a letter to the king asking for a living allowance, which King Mongkut Abdul Kader graciously granted. Tengku Abdul Kader received the requested amount of 300 baht per month. After that, he moved his family to live in the state. He remained in power until his death in 2476.

In 1947, Tengku Abdulkar Mahiyaddin, the 7th son, was the youngest son of Phraya Wichitphakdi or Phraya Tani or Tengku Abdulkader Kamaruddin, who was convicted during the reign of King Chulalongkorn. King Rama V and received kindness from His Majesty and from His Majesty King Mongkut Klao Chao Yu Hua, received money to support their lives and migrated to the city of Kelantan in Malay. He established the Pattani Association (Gabongan Melayu Raya-Gampar) or in Thai, called Kampar. Its head office is in Kota Baru, Kelantan and it has branches in Kedah, Perlis, Pinang and Singapore to implement political policies. For Pattani State

Due to the truly uncaring nature of the government officials, who are corrupt, exploitative, unfair and selective, and the fact that the transportation routes are far from the real centers of power, it is difficult to govern from a centralized location. Most importantly, there are differences in culture, language, religion, traditions and social psychology. The Malay-Thai sway was more towards the Malays than the Thais. Therefore, when the opportunity arose to open up the southern vassal states, namely Pattani, Trang, Kantan, Saiburi and Perlis, to be strong or to be instigated by foreigners, they immediately separated and refused to be under Siamese rule.

Therefore, King Chulalongkorn graciously ordered the administration to be divided into 2 phases. In the first phase, there will be a problem with the old city lords who lost their power because they were dismissed by royal command. He appointed 7 city lords to govern themselves by their own lords, especially the Pattani city lord, who had more influence than anyone else because of his ancient importance. Therefore, the problem of Pattani city lords taking advantage of people arose. Others were always sued until being punished by the land. And in the second period, B.E. 2449

His Majesty graciously ordered the improvement of the administration again by establishing Pattani Province in B.E. 2449 and determined the administrative policy of the 7 provincial governors, which can be summarized as follows:

1. Establish a governance system that is in line with the social and psychological conditions in all dimensions to avoid mental shocks by allowing for relaxation according to Islamic principles if it is a family matter, such as inheritance cases.

2. Select people who are virtuous, selfless, and knowledgeable, including those who can adapt well to Islamic society because they understand the Muslim mind well enough to govern.

3. Accelerate the development of the economy, education, transportation, and public health to be better than the southern capitals under British rule to create comparisons.

4. If the original governor is still alive, he will take care of the city and maintain the status of the governor but increase the cost of living to the point of being able to live perfectly. But when the governor is gone, the city should be merged with other cities, such as in the case of 1916, 4 provinces were merged: Pattani, Sai Buri, Yala and Narathiwat. And in 1931, Pattani Province was dissolved, reducing Sai Buri to a district. It depends on Pattani province. But the important thing during the colonization period was to solve the problem of British threats, but had to give up territories such as the states of Saiburi, Kalantan, Trangan and Perlis to the British as a buffer and to protect them. The British came to instigate these cities to be strong, and the British hoped to intervene. With the force of arms in March R.S. 127 or B.E. 2451 and the reign of King Mongkut Klao Chao Yu Hua, His Majesty graciously ordered Somdet Phra Chao Yukhon Dhighamporn, Prince of Lopburi Ramesuan, to come out and hold the position of Uparaja who was the regent of the southern provinces to control and take care of those provinces closely, as if creating a Prosper according to the principles of King Rama V (Rama V Doctrines)

The results of the reform of the government and the implementation of the 4 principles of the Lord Buddha were able to reduce the problems and unrest in various forms, especially political instability and political, diplomatic and social psychological confusion until the change of government in 1932, but the main policies of King Rama V did not change much.

At the same time, the Malays and Chinese in the Malay Peninsula began to think of declaring independence from the British, just like India, Burma or Vietnam in French Indochinese, which made the idea of Pattani's strength directionless because it did not know whether it would depend on Malay or be an independent state itself because of the influence of the independent states on many groups. Because originally, the British were the bad guys, but later, the British had to protect themselves from the Malay-Chinese nationalism process, and the Malay-Chinese communist-socialist idea was born that wanted to declare the Malay government as a communist socialist state.

When World War II, or the Great East Asia War, broke out, the government of Field Marshal Plaek Phibunsongkhram accepted the Japanese proposal to become an ally and declared war on the ally, allowing the British to support Tengku Muhammad Yatdin, son of Tengku Abdul Kader, the former ruler of Pattani who was dismissed from government service by the royal command of King Rama V, with the Bangkok government. In order for the British to use it as a tool to create a defense line, The Japanese army did not invade the British in Malaya and Singapore by separating the territories of the 3 Thai-Malay border provinces into the Pattani state because Pattani has a river. Therefore, it is a strategic point that the British wanted to use as a naval base to protect the northern frontier to protect the Japanese army.

This strategy, Luang Praditmanutham or Than Pridi Banomyong wrote in the article "Observations on National Unity and Democracy" about Tengku Muhammad Yaddin that "A Free Thai told me (Than Pridi) that in Delhi, India, there was a group of English One held a party to honor this Tengku and called him 'Long live The King of Pattani'". In addition, some political parties in Malaysia provided support to the nationalist movement, which was responded to by Muslims with political ideologies, such as Tengku Yala Na Sae, the son of Phraya Suriyasunthon, the former ruler of Sai Buri.

After Tengku Muhammad Yaddin's death, various movements emerged, such as the violent Muslim separatist movement, the Malay Communist Party, and the Communist Party of Thailand, which had different ideologies but shared a common goal: to undermine the stability of the Thai government. The major separatist movements began with the Malay Communist Party. The National Liberation Front of Pattani (BNPP) is a separatist organization that was established five decades ago, making it an old group with an ideology that dates back to 1947 when the British were about to grant independence to the 9 Malay states, ruled by a Sultan. Each king ruled for 5 years, and at that time, Pattani was able to separate and become independent and established as Pattani State with the King of Pattani State and not directly under any country but received patronage from the neighboring Muslim countries.

This idea made Tengku Muhammad Yaddin use the old ideas of the past. But, it was a separation of territory instead of declaring independence for the benefit of the nation. Because the idea is the most important, the organization was established openly in 2490, using the Malay name Gabon. Gan Melayu Patani Raya has the Pattani National Association or Kampar and has its headquarters in Kota Bharu, Kelantan, and branches in Kedah, Perlis, Pinang, Singapore and Kampar. Its main leaders included Haji Sulong Toh Mina, Haji Sulong bin Abdul Kader and Adul Na Saiburi, former members of the House of Representatives. During 2480–2481, he was the son of Phraya Suriya Sunthon Bovorn Phakdi, the former ruler of Saiburi. He mobilized and encouraged the masses to create a cause. Unrest in the southern region continued intermittently from then on until Tengku Muhammadyaddin died in 2496.

And in the following year, Mr. Haji Sulong Toh Mina also died, causing the Camp to weaken and gradually disintegrate. But in 1977, Mr. Adul Na Saiburi looked at Thai politics in 1957. There was a power struggle between the group of Field Marshal P. Pibulsongkram, the group of Police General Phao Sriyanont, and the group of Field Marshal Sarit Thanarat, and the Cold War began to succeed. The central politics were weakened, so the ideology was continued by gathering More violent than the first era, establishing the terrorist group, the United Front of the National Liberation Front of Pattani, which is a political internationalist fashion to separate Themselves to be independent because in this movement, there are members who have studied in Egypt, such as Mr. Annan Umaydah, and it is considered a group of intellectuals who have succeeded The first era of foreign education led to both political and military movements, which were armed forces fighting against government soldiers and government officials. However, it was later overthrown by the government of Field Marshal Sarit Thanarat, who staged a coup. The government of Field Marshal P. successfully suppressed the country severely, causing chaos and the lack of strong leadership for a period of time.

While Field Marshal Sarit Thanarat was Prime Minister in 1958, there was pressure and suppression against three groups that were enemies of the state:

– Communist Party group or alliance or liberal group that attacks the dictatorship Military

– Group 2 is the anti-government group or the old power group that thought of overthrowing the Sarit system, such as the 1 December 1958 rebellion, in which Air Chief Marshal Sarit and his group were arrested, but the court dismissed the case.

– and the last group is the separatist movement group in the 3 southern border provinces that the government has suppressed with strong military and police force, no different from suppressing the Communist Party or groups that have been accused of destroying the entire nation, including those accused of setting fire and smuggling

There was a decisive use of force in the political situation during the governments of Field Marshal Sarit Thanarat and Field Marshal Thanom Kittikachorn. They used measures to mix in foreigners by moving a large number of people from the Northeast into the South, which led to conflicts in culture and ways of life that lacked understanding, as well as injustice because Thai Muslims were treated as second-class citizens. Because of the dictatorial government, The military sent low-ranking officials from the central government to work in the 3 southern border provinces as punishment, but it gave the Isan people an opportunity to do rough work more easily, so they tried to please the Isan people, which increased their dissatisfaction. However, the strength of the separatist movement at that time was not strong until the Muslim world Changed political direction and used oil as a bargaining power in 2516 When the oil-exporting Arab states did not send oil to the countries that supported Israel in the Yam Kippur War.

Since then, the Israeli nation began to support the Muslims who were few and did not receive justice, including the Thai separatist group who received money from Libya. However, Khunying Saengdao Siamwalla traveled to explain to Libyan leader Col. Gaddafi about the principles of governance and the kindness of His Majesty the King towards the Muslims of Thailand, and he is also the head of the Supporting all religions. Col. Gaddafi stopped supporting terrorism. Separatism during Gaddafii's time, Libya changed to support the Islamic Foundation for Social and Economic Development of Thailand and the Orphanage Foundation of the Thai Muslim Women of Thailand under Royal Patronage, which is considered a show of patriotism and the desire for the world and Thailand to be peaceful. The happiness of Khun Ying Saengdao Siamwalla is truly something that must be praised.

However, there were foreign Muslim private sectors that supported the secession process until the end of the Cold War. The world situation changed because the Soviet Union was destroyed. But the Arab world was revived by the victory of the Afghan Mujahideen against the Soviet Union forces, and the Muslim world movement focused on Palestine, which in the 1970s was marked by violent acts such as hijackings, massacres and bombings of aircraft, including a plot to seize the Israeli Embassy in Thailand in 1972, which General Chatichai Chu Mr. Khunhawan Rattanachai, Deputy Minister of Foreign Affairs, together with Air Chief Marshal Thawee Chultharap, Chief of Staff of the Armed Forces, resolved the situation peacefully. However, one thing that was proven was that the international terrorist act against Israel and the West at that time had no relation with the separatist movement in the three southern provinces.

However, the violence in the form of terrorist bandits still appeared in the area. Pattani and Narathiwat provinces are the majority.

During the period between 1975 and and 1983, General Han Leenanont, the commander of Region 4 at that time, announced the "Cool Under the Shade" policy upon assuming the position and had a deep understanding of the southern problems, including the strategies, tactics, and various political procedures. The military that the separatist group wants to seize the 3 southern border provinces as well as the 1997 Constitution to allow the political strategy to achieve results faster according to the democratic system because Thai people in these 3 provinces are Muslims, more than 80 percent so entering the administration of the sub-district administrative organization is an easy matter for the separatist leaders and announced a hidden strategy on the matter of separating traditions The cultural bond between the two religions of Thai people has existed since ancient times, but it has been broken.

When Thai youth who are Muslims have been forbidden from discussing or participating in activities with Thai Buddhists for almost 20 years, and according to the analysis of General Han Leenanont in the article Stop the Southern Fire Part 2, and as a Senator of Satun Province, he has explained to the Thaksin Shinawatra government the way to create hatred, blocking Thai Buddhist and Thai Muslim youths by citing sin if they speak Thai or read Thai books.

But the principle of the Cold Under the Umbrella that General Han has set has been continued. It will make the situation less severe. At that time, the principles of politics, society and culture were used. According to the principle of coexistence, leading the way to the suppression of emotion, the Cold Under the Umbrella was successful. This is in line with the policy of the government of General Prem Tinsulanonda, who announced the principle of solving the problem in Southern Border Provinces By establishing the Southern Border Provinces Administrative Center or SBPAC, which is the leader in suppressing violence with armed forces since January 20, 2504

Later, on April 23, 2539, the role of the Southern Border Provinces Administrative Center was set to be similar to the frontline government, acting as the main representative of the central government in order to understand the problems and solve them promptly and in an integrated manner, to arrange knowledgeable and capable people to work in the 3 southern border provinces, and to transfer civil servants who did not work effectively. And remove all bad behavior from the area, allowing the Southern Border Provinces Administrative Center to have personnel such as Mr. Plakorn Suwannarat Ongmontri, who at that time held the position of Deputy Minister of Interior but became the Southern Border Provinces Administrative Center Director, so he had the power to coordinate effectively, while at the same time being decisive in governing and having excellent judgment in making decisions to solve the cause of violence.

In the case of Gen. Kitti Ratanachaya, former commander of Region 4, who insisted that before 1995, the Southern Border Provinces Administrative Center (SBPAC) was successful, causing the intensity to decrease, so there was a policy adjustment that became a weak point of the government because it caused the structure and the solution to change or the intensity of the pressure on the violent groups to decrease as well. However, the Southern Border Provinces Administrative Center still performed its duties perfectly and was able to reduce the expansion of the separatist forces to some extent. When the pressure of the military, especially the Marine Department, which is the main force of the 43rd Battalion, pressed and wiped out the separatist guerrillas in the jungle, the important thing is the continuity and the relationship between the intelligence information and tactical methods that are complete and effective, allowing them to pressure the leaders of many groups, especially the new Pulo group, to flee to Malaysia and pursue honest careers elsewhere.

Until April 30, 2545, the Thaksin Shinawatra government adjusted the strategy in the 3 southern border provinces by ordering the Prime Minister's Office to dissolve the Southern Border Provinces Administrative Center and Police Lieutenant Colonel 43 following the recommendation of Pol. Gen. Sant Srutanon, the national police chief on March 30, 2545, which had the phrase "petty thieves" that caused confusion and failure to the government.

And the worst thing is that the responsibility for suppression is transferred to the police instead, most of whom are city police and cannot work with the Border Patrol Police because they act in a way that overshadows the military. In addition, the provincial police use a catch-the-bandits strategy to collect heads because many of the terrorists already have heads, so there is a sham. Murder for reward money causes the intelligence operation to disappear along with the terrorists' lives instead of using the suspects to expand the intelligence results in a tactical way.

The author recalls a historian's remark that "The world is never free from war." This is because humans are born to fight to live according to nature. Humans always think that they can overcome nature and control it, or even... Thinking that he can control animals and the world, he kills animals cruelly to survive. Animals fight against human actions, but most of the time, humans win. However, sometimes nature takes revenge on humans in various forms, such as the case of a severe natural disaster at sea called a tsunami, a major earthquake in China, or a tropical storm in Burma. All of them have caused great destruction to mankind, and mankind has never realized that these natural disasters are all caused by human behavior or that it is fate.

Report from the managing newspaper in collaboration with the Center for Global Relations Institute of Asian Studies, Chulalongkorn University on the Sichuan Geological Disaster Is it fate or mankind?

The tremors were felt in Bangkok on the afternoon of Monday, May 12, 2008, forcing office workers in several central business districts to run for shelter outside their buildings, not expecting that this was just the tail end of the quake, which was about 2,000 kilometers away.

At 14:28 local time, a 7.8-magnitude earthquake struck Wenchuan County, about 92 kilometers northwest of Chengdu City, Sichuan Province, and lasted about 80 seconds. It ripped 33 kilometers deep from the ground and was followed by dozens of 5.0–6.0 aftershocks. Chinese authorities expect The death toll and missing people are expected to exceed 80,000, affecting the lives of 10 million people.

The Earth's plates move. They move and move.

Every time a disaster occurs, the question everyone asks is what caused the tragedy that has brought sorrow to China's most powerful earthquake in 30 years," said Zhang Guomin, a researcher at the Center for Earthquake Forecasting and Research. Shallow-focus earthquakes, which cause tragedy. The damage was huge. In addition, Wenchuan is located in the Longmenshan Fault, which has a high probability of causing earthquakes.

Professor Wang Erxi, an expert from the Institute of Geophysics Research of the Chinese National Social Sciences, explained the cause of the earthquake as the Indian plate moving north collided with the Eurasian plate, which has the Tibet Plateau to the south, causing it to rise eastward and press the Sichuan Basin, which caused the earthquake.

This disaster, if we were to blame only on nature, would be too easy to conclude. Because we all depend on the resources on Earth with every breath. The world is becoming more volatile and erratic every day. Therefore, it is difficult to deny that humans are involved. Some people even conclude that this earthquake and natural disaster, The current fate of humanity is a punishment from the great force of nature.

Mr. Yang Yong, a famous Chinese geologist and conservationist, revealed that the construction of several hydropower dams on the Minjiang River, upstream of the Yangtze River, has caused changes in the geological structure, which is the main cause of this major earthquake. This is because the Minjiang River is located on the China seismic belt. Wenchuan County is located in the buffer zone between the Tibetan Plateau and Sichuan Basin, while the Menjiang River is located on the **"Longmenshan."**

Sadly, the information was warned by the Chinese government several years ago, hoping to seriously review and study the impact of China's large-scale hydropower construction, but all parties have remained indifferent and continued to build hydropower stations to accelerate the country's development. The engine is running at full speed.

According to studies by Western geophysicists, the melting of polar ice caps is related to the generation of earthquakes, as has happened in the past. In Alaska and Canada, on the other hand, ice caps have the ability to prevent earthquakes.

Although there is no proof that human water has created the world's fate in many forms, such as global warming, which has caused polar ice to melt at a terrifying rate, or the construction of large and small dams scattered along the Chang River, Will Jiang be the cause of the 80-second massacre in the 88 days before the Olympics on August 8, 2008? But because everything in the world depends on each other, what happened proved that we are all in the "clutch" of nature's fate.

Why are humans so ignorant and have no wisdom to learn the truth? Nature kills human life as punishment for harming nature. Because humans must fight to defeat each other on this earth. If a small fight is a fight within a family, it is called an internal fight. But if the fight expands to a group, This fight is called a rebellion.

But if the fight expands to involve many sectors of society, such a fight is called a riot. If it causes unrest within the country, it is called a civil war. But if it is a fight between countries, we call it a war, such as the World War, the Vietnam War, the Lebanese War, the Arab-Israeli War, the Falklands War, the Iraq War, etc.

Terrorism is another form of war, no matter what it is called. The loss of life day after day, month after month, year after year, has been, for decades, centuries, happening to the author's hometown, which is located in the three southern border provinces, where our families, our relatives, our brothers and sisters, our friends, our people in these provinces. We were killed and slaughtered without knowing the exact reason. We were so busy fighting for our livelihood, taking care of our children, taking care of our wives, taking care of our friends, and taking care of our relatives, brothers and sisters. We didn't even have time to open up and know who else was suffering, like the southern families.

Even the government itself seems to not understand and is not sincere in solving the problem, but in practice, government officials do not do their job as well as they should, do not help or prevent villagers from being harmed, killed, or may not even pay attention.

As happened to the author's family about 40 years ago, teachers in the southern border provinces had to sacrifice their lives to terrorist groups, killing and destroying the lives and property of teachers, soldiers, police officers, and government officials, including monks, which has happened before and will happen again.

Asked whether the government had run out of medicine and whether the families of the unfortunate people received sufficient compensation and assistance from the government as much as they had first-hand experience. In the case of the writer's brother, who was murdered, the government did not extend a hand to provide assistance as much as it should. It was painful for those who suffered.

5
The government is urgently trying to extinguish the smoke from the southern fires.
To bring it to a close as soon as possible.

Everything has changed according to its nature. Nature is something that arises and changes because everything is it. It is a self that is "Anattamman," which is impermanence, without substance, without self according to the characteristics of the three characteristics of the Buddha that he has declared. Therefore, the world today is increasingly conflicting and competing with each other. Whoever is better or more powerful will have an advantage. Better Opportunity than Advantage To have an opportunity is to have power. Those without power are weak. They will be taken advantage of by the opposite party. There is a need to fight for equality. Fight for yourself. According to the human condition, fighting each other has long-accumulated hatred.

The problem is how to educate and understand the masses of humanity better so that they can connect and connect with each other with compassion and kindness towards humanity on this earth.

This is where we will see that all religions will talk about the "freedom" of human beings. In this human world, there is still oppression, abuse and unfair advantage. On the contrary, there is still a claim in this universe that "Who is the real creator of peace?" Therefore, it is necessary to prove the concept, the behavior, and the teachings that are held. Often appearing in Western media, Is there a new world order, a new world in the 21st century called "New World Order" to create a new peace, real or fake?

Turn to the truth or the truth that humans seek. From birth to death, we will find the truth in life. Those who seek the truth to the point of exchanging their lives, such as Prince "Siddhattha," have found and pointed out to us Know and understand 2 truths, the one that is assumed is the ultimate truth of reality (Reality of reality) and the truth that is assumed (Mundane reality)

This assumed truth is the problem. The truth that is in the darkness. And then try to turn the darkness into the bright truth. But then we are stuck in the assumed truth. That is why the world is destroyed. There is a problem because we are so stubborn. Therefore, we cannot switch ourselves off. We have no chance to reach the ultimate truth. If we reach the ultimate truth, we will live together in freedom. The suffering Ours, the world's heat will not occur.

The heat is a global problem that exists because we cling to imaginary identities. For example, we call ourselves by different names. Some people call themselves by imaginary names such as "Buddhism," "Islam," "Christ," "Hindus," etc.

This is the name of the ideology that we have assumed to call the name because it is convenient in conversation only, nothing more than that. If we do not think firmly in this body, human problems will be almost nonexistent, or there will be very few. The peace that we seek will have a chance to occur in our human society. Suppose that this nation Suppose that the national flag This country, this country, imagine a person who is imagined as a leader, such as the King, the President, the Prime Minister, etc., then we take the imaginary person as the person to act on. It is all just a symbol. Symbolism is just a name or symbol, but we firmly hold on to it. It has become a problem, becoming a war, destroying the peace and freedom of What is human beings? We must understand it clearly. Turn to speak: A hypothetical group of people in the world is hypothetically called "Muslims." All those who call themselves Muslims and join together are called the "Muslim world." He tried to find his symbol. The way of life of Muslims or Muslims must live with honor only. Must make it a person who can live high.

Therefore, we must honor our children and grandchildren. Human beings are the most honorable beings. Honor and dignity must be with Muslims and not Muslims. The question is, how do we live in order to live honorably? Human beings must be taught, trained, and refined to have honor in a spiritual way. The soul by itself that comes from God is not arrogance, boastfulness, arrogance, or the arrogance of mankind. Linking to the great powers of the Western world and the United States

Muslims believe that no one is greater than anyone else. Human problems arise from the invasion of a larger force that considers itself a superpower. What is the purpose of the United Nations (UN)? To create peace for the suffering humanity. Among its members that are not really large, there are only 5 nations that are greater than the others. They are superior to the nations. Others are the world's masters, which Islam does not accept. The world's masters are their own masters, except for Allah alone. There is nothing more sacred than Allah. The more colonial power a powerful country has, the more countries that do not have power are in their control and oppress themselves, and the more power they will have. With the world's masters, this is one point and a big point that Muslims are not satisfied with and Hate superpowers, especially the United States.

Therefore, in the colonial era of the Western empires, which began from 1800 onwards, the West occupied most of the territories of the Islamic world. Almost all Muslims are in the Colonial Era, which is an invasion to occupy territories and resources, bring materialism and occupy the souls with Jewish and Christian Bible teachings. Leading to Rationalism and Materialism, creating a relationship with God.

Then came the flow of materialism to create progress. Following Western ideology, there was criticism of the concept of Secularism. This concept is About the emergence in the 20th century and developed into the 21st century The aim is to move towards Freedom without borders.

Examples that have been cited as history for politicians, historians, and writers on colonialism include the Korean War, World Wars I and II, and the recent Persian Gulf War. We can, therefore, consider the "American Century" to have ended in political catastrophe. (To control) the economy, society, and culture to the masses, causing the cause to have an impact on the civilization of the Islamic world. As it is said inevitably, we must accept this.

The declaration of the "New World Order" by the United States is a change in power that caused a change in humanity from the hopes and dreams that all human beings want in everything, starting from the issue of freedom, independence, the cause of scientific progress, human rights, to the invasion from the West, such as the case of the Jews and Palestine, who want to assimilate Islamic culture.

Why do we have to do this? Because it will bring in a Western society instead. Muslims consider it an evil to the Muslim world. Development of science, technology, communication, information, and education systems to follow the Western way, which is similar to the case of the southern border conflict of our 3 southern provinces that focused on developing physical budgets in an "Overreach" manner without considering The quality of Islam.

In fact, this reason is the root of the conflict. Initially, Muslims feel that they have become colonies of Thailand and are becoming so every day. In terms of governance, politics, economics, military, and other necessities, the three southern provinces that are inferior cannot be compared with other parts of our Thai land. This is why there is opposition from opposition groups in the form of many groups. The Progressive Youth Movement has killed many thousands of lives, more than the deaths in some wars. It is a daily killing, showing the resistance that is getting stronger by the day.

If the show of power is carried out as a global capitalist, the power leads to the expansion of networks as a condition for the connection, including transnational terrorism, separatism, and the uprising for the Islamic revolution led by some religious groups inside and outside the country. These reasons It is the core of the struggle, including the important thing about human rights is to keep the oath that was made before receiving scholarships for study abroad. "The oath and the pledge are not spoken. Honor is far away." And they will feel irritated if they break their own oath.

These religious leaders and scholars are stubborn people, so they do not want to see the world more broadly. They use the Quran instead of the "Democracy" scripture that people all over the world use, which is to say, they do not accept the laws of the country. Laws of both Thailand and foreign countries must have a judgment that which laws should not be used. They must be studied clearly because sometimes the practice conflicts with the Islamic religious commandments, which most people do not accept because they do not accept the teachings. Training on the use of Thai law and see it as "an unfair law."

This is the condition that led to the Islamic revolution that affected the Muslim world. Western powers, and any nation that takes advantage of Muslims, will destroy Muslims are warn those who are obsessed with materialism to "turn to the principles of their religion. They are fighting for the dignity of Muslims and for the justice that the Prophet has promised. Muslims should be aware of the truth and the reality of doing the Hajj (even sacrificing their lives in the way of Allah).

The Quran has been introduced as a modern constitution in the most extreme way to be a guideline for actual practice or to claim the front of some religious leaders in the situation that has occurred in the 3 southern border provinces of our country of Siam. We have a part in the responsibility to fix it. We cannot just sit and watch any longer.

Therefore, it is a challenge to the religious scholars who have played a role (since the Haji Sulong era) and the political and administrative roles to find a common way to solve the problems, create peace and solve the senseless killings.

We can say that it is a value that has wrong and rude behavior, cruelty like animals, love, lacking compassion for fellow human beings who share the same earth. We are born with one life, one mind, one soul, one spirit, a human being in the same seal and state of being human.

Of course, we are not called Muslims. Muslims and non-Muslims, we are all human beings. We live in the same land, air, and nature and breathe the same air. We must think of ourselves and others as human beings and have some humanity. Not to be slaves to anger and hatred. Or use it as a standard, a tool for life measures. It is a bad and evil path and is unjust on one side. We must live our lives with the truth as Allah teaches us: "Do good and do not destroy the lives of others."

Muslims love the truth, love life, and love others, even if they are not Muslims. We are human beings. We do not just call ourselves Muslims. Muslims are names. Therefore, the name is only fiction. It is not the ultimate self. It is the reality of itself (The Reality of Reality).

What must the state seek? Seek the truth (Reality) and make the truth known, including solving the problem of the decaying culture of Western society, which has been flowing heavily. We should choose what should be accepted, what is appropriate, what is not, and the distribution of wealth to poverty, which includes interest. (Dividend) Islamic Bank of Thailand, including the killing of innocent people: "Monks, women, the elderly, children, infants, pregnant women, and dogs that have done nothing wrong"

Hundreds and thousands of people who committed such evil acts in the killing of many lives must be punished appropriately for their actions because they are illegal and inhumane acts of all nations and languages, giving importance to the creation of unrest with seriousness, without regard for anyone, not giving power or any dark power to dominate, aiming to provide safety in life and property Sin, all the time, the pets of our brothers and sisters in the 3 southern border provinces. Able to distinguish who is right and, who is wrong, who is mistaken in order to prevent the expansion of the country's governance system.

The behavior that has passed in the interim period of Using the policy of the cold umbrella, instilling the realization of being Muslim, instilling the sense of being a true Muslim in the hearts of the Muslim youth in many aspects that are necessary. Such as in terms of moral training learning about the use of force in terms of weapons and spirit for the homeland, which has a history of being Muslim in any era before.

The author has done a lot of research and concluded that the true origin of the original local people in ancient times. However, this world does not belong to anyone. God created it for everyone. Claiming ownership is wrong in the first place. The property does not belong to anyone. God created it for everyone. But later it was hypothetically referred to as inherited as the "Siamese Kingdom" in the end. It is necessary to have a single history that the government must take part in solving the ignorance of Thai society about Muslims, solving public problems of the people on the southern border showing the suspicion, hatred and fear of Muslims and changing the attitude that "Islam is a religion that uses violence."

Therefore, it is the reason that causes the Thai society in the southern region to be divided into two sides. One side is Thai Buddhist, and the other side is Thai Muslim. The division between Thai Buddhists and Thai Muslims is a failure of the government to eliminate the ignorance and misunderstanding of the Muslimness of Thai society.

This is the reason why most Thais are in the dark, confused, under the "problem of ignorance" until it becomes suspicion and hatred. In the case of the incident at the Krue Se Mosque in Pattani Province on April 28, 2004, the media explained that the actions of this group of Muslim youths were a religious duty, which is "Hajjir" or holy war. Or what the general public calls the "Suicide War" or "Sahid" (those who were killed on the religious battlefield at the hands of the infidels)

The government and academics must study deeply and truly the Malay society, Malaysia, Malaysia, Indonesian society, etc., to strengthen the cultural power and coexistence to be used for the benefit of the southern region of Thailand. The government must honor the dressing choices of Muslims, which is part of the tradition, namely, give more freedom to Muslim women according to the principles of Muslim women, even in other places such as Europe (France, Greece) etc. They wear hijab because they have a sense of being Muslim. In the land of Muslims, which is more correct, in the southern part of the country, Thailand, we are the same because of the inspiration for the dignity and justice of Muslims as in the present.

What influence do Muslims have on Muslim people in the South? Let's study it carefully. We will find that some religious scholars have said that Some Islamic countries should not fall into the hands of religion. But in fact, Islam is a religion that has the teachings of God. In the same way, America, Europe, South America, Africa, and even some parts of Asia, these countries believe in the Bible. Because his country has been holding on to Christianity as the main religion as part of our Thai society. Muslims believe in the teachings of God, which include politics and governance.

Therefore, praying together on Friday is good, praying together is good, but politics are mixed with religion. Of course, the act of worship, but politics and worship are mixed together. Some people try to separate religion from politics. Religious teachers play a role in politics and governance. Therefore, Muslims in the southern region of Thailand will probably Certainly not want to be the ruler himself but have a role (i.e., have a role, participate, be involved)

For this reason, the author believes that only religious leaders can incite the people in the southern region to sacrifice for peace in this region. Why… Because Muslim people are willing to pay attention to and listen to religious leaders. The government must understand that religion plays a part in politics. Politics plays a part in religious society, such as the society in the Islamic world, like our southern region. Clearly and clearly

Because the people are willing to pay attention to and believe in the religious leaders of the Thai Muslims in the South, they understand well or the total belief that the religious leaders have good intentions for the Thai Muslims in the three southern border provinces to have a population that will increase gradually.

Originally, the ratio of Buddhists to Muslims was about 18:82 (Buddhist % Muslim %?) 2-3 years ago, but now the ratio has changed to 15:85. Therefore, it is very important that the government consider and examine the environment and must urgently clean up the Islamic education that plays a part in the creation And to emphasize peace in line with religious principles, sending mercy to the universe among Muslims around the world, believing that Islam will remain permanently and will not fade away from this world, and that Islam alone will be the last religion left in the world.

The Islamic religious structure adheres to Islamic law, the Islamic way of life, and Islamic Dharma (the truth is no different from Buddhists who believe that living and following Buddhist traditions is based on Dharma). However, what is different is that Islam teaches people to create enemies, kill themselves, and sacrifice their lives to wage war. Buddhism teaches about loving-kindness and compassion. Like Christianity, God loves everyone, including Buddhism and Islam. But Islam has been transformed into a brutal form of hatred and cruelty towards non-Islam. This is the difference that is apparent from other religions.

The special characteristic of Muslims in the 3 southern border provinces in the past is that they want to continue their lives in the Islamic way and have a desire not only to change the form of governance, politics and economics but also to participate in changing every aspect of the Muslim people's way of life from bad things to good things and including changing their values. The behavior and behavior of the government, civil servants or representatives who are immoral, look down on Muslims as second-class citizens, have no morality, are not fair, do not respect Muslims, corruption, etc., must be completely eliminated. Change the ethics of the people.

Many movements have been organized in the past, from one government to the present government, to create and develop the level of knowledge and understanding of Islam to reduce the gap of religious, cultural and ethnic differences that are mostly Malay (not meaning to assimilate the nation, religion and traditions but to link them together) Integrate into Multicultural Like Dr. Martin Luther King successfully developed between blacks and whites in the United States.

The government must use valuable examples from the successful minority leaders in the past in the 3 southern border provinces of Thailand to achieve the sense of being brothers and sisters of the same religion, who can discuss and lead to unity or be brothers and sisters of the whole world together. Why…? Because everyone lives in this world together. "Islam is a global thing." It is a universal, far-sighted religion. Therefore, grading religions will make it a narrow thing. Don't lower the level of Islam. But don't let your own narrow worldview block the way of religion because Islam is a religion that is about all human beings…

So, what should a religious person have? A religious person must be full of love and kindness. Islam is a religion that creates people to be humble and humble towards everyone. Therefore, Islam condemns terrorism both in Thailand and abroad (outside the country), condemns the use of violence to solve problems, and condemns violations. Rights Therefore, if a person believes in it, he will attain peace. A person who has truth reaches truth and will attain "peace." And is it impossible for religion to teach the use of violence? Terrorism war is the last resort, the last tool to achieve victory. And when victory is achieved, peace can be created.

So, what should a religious person have? A religious person must be full of love and kindness. Islam is a religion that creates people to be humble and humble towards everyone. Therefore, Islam condemns terrorism both in Thailand and abroad (outside the country), condemns the use of violence to solve problems, and condemns violations. Rights Therefore, if a person believes in it, he will attain peace. A person who has truth reaches truth and will attain "peace." And is it impossible for religion to teach the use of violence? Terrorism war is the last resort, the last tool to achieve victory. And when victory is achieved, peace can be created.

A world of change in the South

The author is very concerned that the situation in the 3 southern provinces that have been smoky both in the past and present has a context of the global situation (External pressure) and the existence of the stability factors that have accumulated and mixed together significantly. The solution to the new problem of the state (the current government) must be very careful, meticulous and detailed, more than the usual solution. Because in the past, every case, every event seemed like solving problems like a childish, ignorant, and absent-minded person. It was due to a sudden emotion. So, it was the power of anger that took over the heart. We had to use a lot of wisdom for how can solving problems in a sudden emotion be effective? In addition to leading the state into a "war trap" with the most extreme and wrong process of the state, which is like a very deep and mysterious situation, the state cannot withdraw or what is called digging its own grave.

The author has summarized the events that have been studied for decades until the current events are the cause of the fire under the sky, the sparks, the smoke, the fire is increasing, almost like a land of war. It is almost a world war because we have seen the path of history that has already happened in this century. No government in the past has been able to solve the problem of the fire under the sky.

If the government of General Prayut Chan-o-cha is lucky, it seems that it will start to turn its direction in terms of being serious about solving this problem, following the guidelines that have been practiced. If we can solve the southern insurgency problem, no matter what form or condition, whether it is a political strategy, civilization, or any resolution, it may not be successful or bring about any "success" with the southern insurgency problem. Or the problem of Muslims and Muslims all over the world, with Thai people and of the powerful nations, including Europe and America, after the 9/11 incident, we can see that the world situation has a connection with the southern part of Thailand, as we cannot deny.

The world situation and the problems of southern Thailand

The South is not an independent country, meaning it does not exist in a separate area. The world situation reflects the South. The conflict situation of the Western superpowers, which is currently flowing into the Muslim world (Arab World) on the stage that is currently fighting between countries (Thailand), the reader must understand that it reflects the impact by implication. Directly to the perspective of Thai brothers and sisters Muslims in Thailand in the 3 southern border provinces, which is called unavoidable at all

The result of this conflict is considered to be a matter between America and the Muslim world, but it reflects the worldview of Muslims in the 3 southern border provinces, which has been multiplied by politicization because this group of people may not only oppose the United States but may also oppose the government's policies that support the United States. Including the Thai government

Muslims have come to hate the part that supports the Thai government, which has become a force that accelerates the incitement of the incident, with the smoke and sparks that have risen as a force that continues to because it is like a tsunami that the government cannot suppress until there is no good policy direction that can control the incident that is happening at present, in a way that will bring about peace.

Let's look at the current struggle between the West and the Muslim world on the world stage that is causing great damage to humanity, our fellow human beings, by making some Muslims turn to a more "religious fundamentalist" tradition. This view is not enough. At the same time, it has been led to have a "very radical view." "Radicalization" as it has occurred and continues in the three southern border provinces of Thailand every day.

When we observe the reality of the situation that happened, it is not a new thing. It is an old thing being reborn. The old thing is made new. Because in the world political arena, we have already experienced something like this, such as World War II (WWII). Thailand also participated. Later, the war between the Soviet Union and the Muslim volunteers hosted by Afghanistan became the stage for the war. In addition, the events occurred in the context of the "Cold War" and during this period, the United States also fully supported the Mujahideen fighters on the Afghan battlefield, just as the West once supported President Saddam Hussein of Iraq in his war against the "Israeli government of Iran."

Sunset vs. Muslim

We have just experienced the "context" of the current situation, which is different. As a result of the events of September 11, 2001, it is the root cause of the conflict between the West and the Muslim world (West V. Muslim world) has expanded widely and rapidly, beyond our imagination or our calculation.

Therefore, the conflict as described in the above incident does not exist only in the context of the US vs. the Muslim world but also in the context of a symmetrical society that has emerged, starting from both the US interest point and the old case between Iran and Palestine and has had an impact.

Therefore, we may combine the current world into two worlds: the internationalist world and the Islamic world dimension. Such stories, in summary, are reflections of the political changes in the world where the ideological war has ended, but the civilization war is occurring. One may ask whether the civilization war should involve negotiation and compromise for peace rather than killing each other like a war. This is the creation of stability and the solution to the southern insurgency.

We both have to admit that it is not easy, General… In the southern region, there are southern fires blazing and spreading as much as at present, such as the Communist Party era and the land seizing movement, but the war can end the southern problems and ease up as if there is nothing (the source is a conversation between General San Chitpatima and Dr. Sompong Dumdeang).

To summarize further, all the above, including the new episodes to accept the new changes, do not follow the new people, drink only the new, the new people are good people, have new perspectives, new worldviews, new knowledge, new understanding, new organizations (to join with the new people, such as new strategies, to be the most prepared), and the new management must be directly involved in the creation of **"New culture."**

How to integrate Islam with Buddhism in a society called a dialogue or a reconciliation When there was a funeral of a younger brother, a younger brother, a mother's funeral, or a father's funeral, there were more than 50 Muslim brothers and sisters attending the Buddhist temple. Because he was dressed in Western clothes, the writer did not know that he was Muslim, so he invited him to go up and offer a robe to the family. He apologized. He was a Muslim and could not do it. He came because of the goodness of the deceased. The writer is very happy and delighted because they discussed and reconciled with Thailand. We should find new cultural principles and use them as examples in southern society to get a new culture of problem management that must lead to having a master, unity, and joint practice.

This is an attempt to present a solution to the problems of the southern border provinces. The author would like to reiterate that it is an acceptance of the ears, seeing with the eyes that what happened has expanded into a disease, spreading from the wound of the disease of the conflict from the Western world to our continent, Western Asia. For example, the events in the Philippines and the MILF in Indonesia are clear witnesses and signals of the movement of the war movement. This is especially true when the global government cracks down on terrorist networks in Singapore, including The arrest of leaders like Hambali in Ayutthaya Province in Thailand and handing them over to the US also reinforces the initial signal already described.

The description or mention of the problem of unrest in the southern border provinces, even for ordinary people, clearly shows that it is a factor from outside, playing a role in the internal problems of Thailand. It will not become an opportunity and a condition for actors from outside the stage to become a new role in the villages of our 3 southern border provinces.

Therefore, the political characters of the Thai state that are related to the political characters outside have a role in connecting and communicating with the situation on the part of the traditionalist "terrorist" group alone is not enough. If it does not become a channel for the superpowers to come and make the southern part of Thailand

For example, when Obama visited Thailand and Burma, Khun Yingluck Shinawatra showed behavior in the form of kneeling and running, begging Obama to help. The unrest in the 3 southern border provinces of Thailand, both in terms of the economy, military, politics, etc., from the United States clearly. The image that the media of Khun Yingluck showed of Obama, the President of the United States, was an image that was disgusting and disgusting to those who I have seen and followed a lot.

Therefore, the South has become a battlefield of a small war. It is the cause of thousands of local lives being lost, with daily killings. It is a very pitiful and sad story that the Southern people are living in an unrestful way. They do not receive justice because of dark powers, both local and political influences, or the world between the "West and the Muslim world."

Managing the Southern Problems, the Problem of Southern Security, we must be mindful and careful in detail throughout the process of solving the problem. We will try not to let the world situation turn the Southern region into a "Civilization War Battlefield."

The word "statehood" in the writer's meaning goes back a little bit. Once upon a time, it was good for the country and the people of the South of Thailand. On the other hand, it caused painful changes for the

Thai Muslims, a group in the southern society that had to take time to heal the heartbreak that had been there for centuries. How likely is it that past administrators mismanaged the welfare of local Muslims and did not meet the needs of local people?

In particular, the rulers and officials of that era used their power and were biased against Muslims, viewing them as lowly and ignorant people, seeing them as second-class citizens, not thinking that they were Thais or Thai Muslims, Thai citizens who were born and lived on the same land, had the same rights, and had the same needs. According to the democratic system, they had the same needs, which caused Muslims to suffer from heartache in the local society. Far away in the area of 3 southern border provinces.

Arresting religious teachers and religious leaders without reason and in a vague manner, which religious leaders are important spiritual leaders, especially in Muslim society, when arresting them without evidence, arresting them randomly because they are respected in society, because they can reconcile the hearts of the Muslims in the South well, like monks in our Buddhism who behave well, behave well, and do good for the country, there will be a large number of Buddhists. Many respect and revere the same, such as in the era of Luang Por Phra Phimon Tham, who is considered the father of Thai monk education, laid the foundation for monks and novices to have a modern and broad world education and was the pioneer of the (Modern Educational System).

The author himself was also influenced by the works of Luang Por Phra Phimontham. Due to the incident when Luang Por Phra Phimontham was arrested, the author was the observer who closely looked after one person every time the court made an appointment. However, in the end, there was no evidence of guilt that could be cited in any way. In the end, Luang Por had to be released and returned to hold the position of "Phra Phimontham."

The evil that happened to Luang Por Phra Phimon Tham in Buddhism How can there be evil deeds and evil intentions toward religious teachers? Muslim religious leaders can do the same. The writer agrees with Muslim brothers and sisters arrested without any evidence (No solid evidence) No justice from the government in almost every era.

The disintegration of the group, the era of Field Marshal P. Pibulsongkram, and the capture of Haji Sulong, The water in the Gulf of Thailand near Koh Nu and Koh Maew was destroyed in a cruel way. It caused the connection of the territorial divisions that continued. Haji Sulong was a leader who wanted that Muslims would receive justice from "statehood" only. If the state of reconciliation governed with compassion like the United States, providing safety Dr. Martin Luther King in America This time, the conflict and disturbance in our 3 southern border provinces has not ended yet. Haji Su is gone.

It is not too late for us to understand, access and develop ways to unite and create peace in the southern region. For example, the government must honor and accept by using a policy of integration in various forms through various processes, such as creating local communities and immigrating Thai Muslims to live and create communities together (like America, creating its own communities for American Indians) Give them capital to invest in casinos, create jobs with evidence For them, the Department of Public Welfare has come to help) The grassroots people are as follows

There are many good examples that people around the world have successfully done and have lived in peace. Thai leaders must open their ears and eyes and bring good beliefs and methods to bring good policies to use in our southern region. We have many social scientists In Thailand, we should bring them to use in our southern region to consult on the issue of The conflict between Thai Muslim brothers and sisters to join the government and civil servants, creating a community of all kinds, including facilities that may differ from the way of life of Muslims, how unlikely is it that there will be different acceptance, and leading to the division that must Need to find the answer together Integration Coherence or Integration of Marriage like the writer's family Respect, trust, fear, trust between 2 groups Thai Buddhist and Thai Muslim society will be one, suspicion will not occur.

On the other hand, most government officials come from the central part of the "state" model. They tend to follow the central policy, according to the administrative power, commanding the local work that can be directly rewarded and punished.

The author observes that government officials at the head of the agency often do not recognize and do not try to understand the differences in society and culture. They also neglect to give study of the social structure, economy, living conditions, and education systems of local grassroots people. They do not understand the mentality and living conditions that cannot be explained as equality.

Mitti and other political movements such as non-discrimination The disdain for the ignorance and lack of understanding of the Thai language of the local Muslims in the South are often seen as "rebellious guests," and other threatening words are used against them that are not beautiful. For example, in Samphanthawittaya School in Cho-airong District, Narathiwat Province, where Mr. Ma-Sae Lu-Seng, a teacher at the school, was searched for evidence of strategic separatism, is one of the suspects in the robbery of weapons of the 4th Development Division. In early 2004, a student in this school went to contact the district office about household registration, and the administrative officer answered that he was a "student thief," which made him feel very embarrassed and sad to the point of crying. This was one of the reasons why they hated government officials because they were branded as thieves even though they were innocent and had no part in being a student thief. Or not, As the government officials claimed.

Therefore, the author would like to suggest to the government, especially the new government of Gen. Prayut Chan-o-cha, that they should be more flexible in using words. Distinguishing behavior is considered a science of "human relations" that must be studied and recognized in conjunction with performing official duties with sincerity. Honesty according to the code of ethics of government officials, management guidelines and governance, and adherence to the principles of law called (Law Enforcement) will be applied in the suppression, arrest, search and arrest of suspects or accused persons whether at home, school, mosque or other places, must be done in a "peaceful manner." Violence should not be used because we are considered to have power in a "Uniform" type of equipment, with weapons in hand, acting arrogantly, showing off, but it may mean decisiveness that must be taken into account and preserved, which may be severe if the situation changes according to the peaceful method. It will make the event have its own relationship.

We need to explain the meaning of "violence" from the perspective of our brothers and sisters. Islam means the fear of having to change "faith." If the meaning is not understood correctly, it may become an infidel, and it is a fear that becomes blasphemy like going to hell, similar to Buddhists who are afraid that if they do only bad deeds, they will go to hell or Christians who are considered disloyal to God or not, if you wash away your sins with God, then your life ahead will go to hell. This is the meaning of the word "severe" for Muslims.

Another thing that the author wants the readers to understand and be aware of is the solution to the unrest in the South, which is the inappropriate dispatch of civil servants to perform their duties. They were sent because they were their own followers. Selfishness, lack of examination of potential, qualifications, quality, ability, understanding of differences, oppression, exploitation, disdain, and disrespect of local people, including discrimination and inefficient allocation of budget resources in terms of economic development, society, and grassroots education. From small children's schools (kindergarten), "Tadika" and Ponoh schools, which have adult students, the elderly, the elderly, orphans, and homeless children, no shelter and food must be relied on "Teacher's Table." The owner of the school, the owner of the hut. They are nurturing and raising their lives to grow in a society called the futureless society, which is a direction of life without a future. According to karma, it seems like an underdeveloped life that is left neglected and uncared for.

However, if they lack the standard of education in all aspects, when they grow up, not having a job will create a bad feeling in the mind. Therefore, some groups of youth have been "brainwashed" and hate government officials without restraint in the community. Poverty, no money because of not having a job. Unemployment, if it is abundant in this southern region, is a cause and a factor of many social problems that will follow.

We, the readers, must not forget that there is no family that provides warmth like a bird flying around in its native land, lacking a permanent shelter. Most of these young people, whom we call "extreme youth," will live in huts, shacks or traditional Pondok schools. While they live in the school Ponoh, they will receive religious instruction similar to our Buddhist traditions, which we call temple children. They may come from different families, such as those with no parents (the parents may have been killed), orphans, or destitute children. Of course, some may volunteer to stay in the temple for education. Our Thai traditions and cultures are different. The monks who support Thai temple children do not have Brain Wash for temple children or the teacher's desk that is done. Because no government agency has come to take care of everything in the current situation.

This is the weak point of the government that does not reach, understand and help develop the youth of the grassroots society, causing a lack of knowledge and skills or may not pay attention or think that it will become a burden for the government. This is a serious mistake. It must be solved quickly. Otherwise, these excessive youth problems will become "conditional" problems that must be solved immediately and urgently. It cannot be left any longer. If the government takes care of and supports, it must speak to each other to understand and accept the society of Muslim brothers and sisters in the 3 southern border provinces.

Youth Remains

Turning to the problem of "the rest of the youth," the problem of "the rest of the youth" can be easily understood as the excess formula is not in the right placeThe remainder-When it comes to humans, the group of "the rest of the youth" is left behind in the society, doing undesirable jobs. There are youth of the writer's generation in the village where the writer spent their early childhood. After completing compulsory primary school, The writer and his brother had the opportunity to continue their education in secondary school (at that time, it was called M.O.R.) My parents did not want me to stay at home and farm. It just so happened that my father, who was a head teacher, suggested that I continue my education for the future. A good opportunity was fortunate.

But many young people of the same generation got low grades, their parents were poor, they had no money to send them to school, they just lived haphazardly, helping their families with rice farming, a little bit of it in a year, when the fifth month of summer arrived, they went out and had fun. Petty theft in the village itself, flirting with girls, having free sex according to the event, having children unexpectedly or planning a family, stealing cows, stealing chickens, stealing pigs, drinking alcohol, getting drunk, playing crazy, playing cards, all of these are disasters. The police and officers are few or almost none. They are young people who have the opportunity to do evil acts illegally. It is a normal event every day because the officers and The police are not taking care of everyone.

This is a social problem that occurs in the rural areas where the author was born. Other rural areas throughout Thailand, which are far from development, are probably not strange for the rural areas where the author grew up. This is the problem of "young people who are left behind." Therefore, very few people receive education to create their own future. However, the chance to go up to a higher education level is even less. 5-10% is already difficult. If there is a movement to encourage Studying abroad in countries like the Arab world, it is easy to make any binding contract that can be signed. Why… Because the environment is so strict, the "young left" is quite easily involved in the process. It is forced by the environment.

Therefore, the remaining youths, when they graduated from overseas studies, returned to Thailand. They had no choice in choosing the direction of life that they wanted, which was to join the movement. The youth "force" had been trained and had a lot of experience. Therefore, the creation of the "daily murder" situation occurred quite often. Freedom to act in a manner known as "guerrilla tactics" or what the French call "**hit and run.**"

Therefore, not only can't the person, but even the news and clues are still not very clear.

To find the powerful people of this era, you have to go down to see the area yourself to know with your own eyes.

Finding news from religious leaders is very difficult. Getting close to Grassroots masses who are not in line with the village headman, headman, or local leader will achieve greater results than if they approached closely, step by step, and use the principle of "Leading politics and military will yield greater results than assessing the situation and acting continuously in a reliable and unbiased manner."

Therefore, the problems in the daily lives of Thai Muslims must first rely on the "Teacher's Table" or the gang or the government officials. The answer is clearer in order. The government's order to raise a large number of forces along with war weapons, as if going to fight and capture the enemy with determination to kill like in World War II.

The author would like to warn that the government does not need to prepare weapons at full force (Basic Load). Use the budget to develop vocational education and training for Thai Muslim youth. The important thing is to understand the dimensions of weapons. Openly implementing weapons will create more friendship and trust. If the government follows the author's suggestions, it will not jeopardize the results of the strategic operation in any way. The search for weapons storage sites in the school of Ponoh is like a suspect of innocent students becoming a dangerous enemy that must be dealt with decisively. Because doubt is a common part of knowing, looting, and burning down the school, it is a concept that shakes the painful feeling and is still in the deep part of the heart, the deep part of the heart throughout life.

The result is that students have now run away to study elsewhere and go to Malaysia until it has become a normal habit that if they face hardship and are oppressed severely by the government, they will turn to rely on Malaysia. This is an event that has been going on for a long time, but the government has not cared and has not found a solution, leaving it like this until today. Or as the government has been advertising that it will solve the problems of the 3 southern border provinces. It's just a lie to the villagers. Which government? Which government has not taken action? Seriously and sincerely, not giving justice to the South, not giving complete freedom to our brothers and sisters in the 3 southern provinces to keep the promises that were made.

The negative effects of abusive behavior

Turning to the actions of government officials, such as the behavior of making slanderous accusations without evidence, without witnesses (no evidence), slanderous accusations It is a great sin to be accused without information, without evidence It creates pain and discredit for the defendant, family, relatives, friends, students, and associates. But looking at it from the other side or the other way around, if the perpetrators have truly committed the crime according to the evidence, of course, it is appropriate. Punish according to the law of the country, regardless of who it is, including politicians or gangsters or influential people or servants of politicians and political parties, locally and nationally, with the hope of becoming a political powerhouse in the future. Such actions and behaviors are a great danger to society in the 3 southern border provinces that cannot be avoided.

The author clearly states his thoughts on the concept of fighting the unrest in the 3 southern border provinces. It comes from the main roots or factors as follows. The author himself sees that the historical roots are the important factors that the government must review the important lessons as the first priority. History is the cause of the unrest in the South as stated in the Buddha's speech. It is said that "hetuppabhava", everything comes from a cause. If the problem solvers, whether politicians, security administrators, sociologists, political philosophers, strategists, humanists, including legal scholars, must know, must understand, must understand "the cause of the current results of the crisis under the problem" clearly. Because the problem under it is a complex problem within itself.

Historical Dimension

Therefore, the author knows well that most Muslims in Thailand are Malays who have settled in the 3 southern provinces. Most of them have developed (Historical Development) and have changed from the state of Langkasuka that used to hold Respect, worship Hinduism, Brahmanism and Buddhism. Around 700-2000 B.E., later became the Islamic State of Pattani Darussalam (2043-2353 B.E.) fought a traditional war with Siam in 2329 B.E. until it became a part of the country of Siam completely since 2445 B.E.

Therefore, learning Thai history focuses mainly on political implications. It is an effect that causes local communities to be neglected, taking other ethnic groups that make up the current Thai nation. In addition, there is also a process of creating a single unity in the nation that neglects the importance of being a small ethnic group, which has unfortunately changed.

Religious Dimension

When looking at religious principles or religious practices or promoting religion in terms of seeking knowledge of Islamic ways to know oneself what one is doing, for whom one is doing it, where one goes after death, how the person who sustains life is happy, in the immortal world after death, including studying to find worldly knowledge as a career to live self-sufficiently and Family to be able to practice religion perfectly according to one's ability and Traditional teaching is the Pondok, teaching students to read the Qur'an, explaining the tithika (religious texts) in mosques, in homes Religious leaders with knowledgeable and experienced teachers called "teacher's table" Many of them who are qualified and of high age are respected as a tradition of The continuous transfer of knowledge and practice has made Muslims in the southern border provinces of Thailand a strong society, a solid and solid society, able to maintain the original community as much as possible, which is a society that is part of the announcement of the "Tokru" institution, so it is the highest institution of Muslims that is very valuable to the Muslim community in the area and in the 3 southern border provinces.

Basic factors of Malay ethnicity

If we agree with anthropologists and historians, we will accept that the Malay ethnicity, which is the majority of the people of the area (the three southern border provinces), and the diversity of races that have arisen are all components of the local people who are Thai people. Logically, the writer includes the total number of races. The origin of Malay people is a race that has a religion, customs, and way of life based on religion and community existence that is different from the majority of Thai people in our country and has been passed down for hundreds of years. It is a dignity that gives great pride and honor to the (different) community. There are children and grandchildren who Inherited until the present, there are religious scholars who have works such as Haji Sulong, religious scholar and political scholar Wan Muhammad Noor Matha, etc., who have created works of religious literature that is not only accepted in the three southern border provinces or the Middle East but are accepted all over the world. This is the outstandingness that has spread and shone brightly in our three southern border provinces.

I would like to summarize for the readers that the idea of fighting the unrest in the 3 southern border provinces will come from the main causes, namely, the lack of education and the poverty. Even foreigners visited the writer's brother's house in Khok Pho. While we were in the border patrol car to visit the writer's brother, the writer's wife's grandmother, Professor Dr. Penny Olsen of the University of Montana was The author was asked a question by economist and agricultural adviser to several U.S. Presidents and the following is a conversation between the author and Dr. Penny.

Dr. Penny: What can these people do for a living? Because it seems that the land in the arid area is quite difficult to live in. You could say that they are very poor. Written: Some are teachers, some are rubber plantations, some are gardeners, some are fishermen, some are taxi drivers, etc., just to make a living each day.

Dr. Penny: I feel like they are having a very difficult life.

Written: If the government takes care of education from the compulsory level In general schools as in other regions, and should have special characteristics that Most people in these 3 provinces speak Jawi or Malay. They can speak, read and write Thai a little, but not very well. When they finish compulsory education, coupled with being strict Muslims and doing religious activities regularly, this is an important factor that is an obstacle to the education of youth who will love the progress in the future and including the understanding in transferring various knowledge to develop knowledge and experience. In addition, there is also a lack of planning to create an understanding of various events environments. The travel of government officials into important areas and places, provincial halls, mosques, and mosques to discuss or hold joint meetings, feels like being in an atmosphere that is different from other parts of the country, for example, the beautiful dresses, neat and tidy traditions such as sarongs, hats, and hijabs, etc.

The people want the government to take care of and support them. The most important thing is people want higher education institutions, very high education so that they will have enough knowledge to be like other Thai society in other regions, so that they will be a basic standard, have permanent jobs, and be able to support themselves, their families, and their children and grandchildren with a standard life like other Thais. They also want a full-fledged university. Complete all majors that foreigners call (Comprehensive University) in the province of Thai Muslim brothers and sisters. Establishing only Prince of Songkla University in Pattani Province is not enough. There should be a university in every province in the 3 southern border provinces. And must focus on fisheries technology, agriculture, communication, humanities, etc.

It should not be focused solely on theology and history, which are considered to be at a very low level and not comparable to world-class universities. The education budget must be doubled. Reduce the budget for strategic or defense spending. Increase the budget for the education ministry. This is the first important factor because: The issue of having a good education will lead to employment, freedom from disease, and a good economy. Having a house to live in, having food to eat, having medicine to cure diseases, etc.

This is the necessity of human beings. Human beings hold on to the 4 requisites to have a place to live. It doesn't have to be as luxurious as Westerners, just have the basics. Medicine, clothing and transportation:

These four things are the foundation of every life that lives together on this earth. The long-term solution to the root cause of the Southern fire is to ask the government to support the establishment of a "university city." It does not have to be a big city or a metropolitan like Bangkok.

The government must support raising the standard of education from young children to higher education to the same standard, register the Pondok schools under the care of special agencies, support them in all aspects, and give them the authority to increase their salary and compensation in the vulnerable areas (Living expense in sensitive Areas) of Pondok school teachers as appropriate.

In addition, the public must participate in determining the university administration's plan to attract philosophies and people from various regions of Thailand and neighboring countries to become students. This is a good factor that will create jobs and generate income for the local area (During the time the author surveyed the average university student expenses, it was approximately 7,000 baht/person/month).

Money is not the main factor or the decisive factor in resolving the unrest in the South. Solving the problem of governance to be "stable" is the first priority. Domestic politics will be strengthened as the next urgent matter in the near future of the South.

Creating a modern university city with all branches of study, focusing on careers, culture, religion, including democracy and the dangers of drugs. It is a hub of civilization, religion and culture, focusing on Peace Studies, Peace Education and Peace Support, including educational curriculum, emphasizing Peace Studies and the role of the process of participation in changing conflicts teaching Peace Studies.

The objective is to reduce the use of violence resulting from conflicts, promote the transformation of conflicts through peaceful methods (Peace Method) and enhance the capacity of individuals, groups, social movements, and institutions to understand the peace movement, including developing skills, values, and knowledge to strengthen the building of a sustainable peaceful society and culture. The basis for promoting peaceful learning

Studying cases from various countries that have differences and conflicts, such as Armenia, India, Philippines, Sri Lanka, Indonesia, etc., can be used as a basis for promoting peaceful learning "in Thailand" and asking the question of whether peaceful learning is an important aspect of learning in Thailand, especially in the 3 southern provinces of Thailand.

Seeking new academics in the form of "interdisciplinary," which is a factor that connects knowledge of social science, humanities, political science, economics and other fields to participate in the analysis for what? To find the root of conflict that occurs in society (not general society) but Thai society and society in the 3 southern border provinces at present to solve the problem without using violence, emphasizing the process. Dialogues for learning between characters who are in conflict with each other To create empathy and change the relationship From confrontation as enemies to mutual respect in the differences, Especially conflicts and violent incidents in 3 southern border provinces of Thailand Conflict due to differences in political ideology, for example, conflicts of the masses Thai Yellow and the Thai Red masses that arose in Thailand, always trying to solve the problem of the overall steps for the peace process.

The government should set a strategy, namely, planning to develop the 3 southern border provinces to have the potential to be a modern university city to be an educational center as it is at Prince of Songkla

University, but it must be adjusted and improved to keep up with the world, keep up with the needs of the current events, including general subjects as previously described. To be both official Study the Islamic religious center in South Asia as much as possible. This problem is the root of all problems.

Border security The state must answer the problem of using the law of the prosecutor. The battle is contrary to the daily killing incident. Even though H.E. Phokin Plukkul held a meeting At the provincial hall, there was a bomb planted at the post office intentionally. The state must be very careful and analyze whether it is an international terrorist process that has connections from abroad or not.

The use of law, judicial law, and criminal law should not be timely because they clearly challenge the authority of the state. The state must organize a small military unit to be inserted as a unit (Stay Behind), a secretive force, with the support of the International Security Act (ISA), such as Malaysia and the United States. Use judicial law as a final step to adjust the mindset of the people in authority.

For example, if the head of the government understands the "ideological" strategy first, it will be easier to solve the problem and be able to trace and answer the question of the disappearance of lawyer Somchai Nilpaichit, president of the Muslim Lawyers Club. Who murdered Khru Piphat Dumdeang, Khru Piphat's comrade-in-arms, Mr. Kiang Chantrat.

When the state has arrested the killer, why did they let him go free? Who has the power over the state officials, the state process, or the state officials who are greedy for money and failed in the case of the killers of Khru Pipat and Mr. Kiang because of corruption? Money is more important than the lives of people who have died for the nation. The law is in the books. The state officials do not care because money alone is the biggest factor in the lives of people. State officials who must be eliminated and other victims must be carried out according to the prescribed justice process because they hope that the law will arrest 9 suspects who robbed guns to cause unrest in the southern region, including a famous MP from Narathiwat Province, who was just arrested during the government of Gen. Prayut Chan-o-cha. If we really arrest them, The current government model will ease the situation quite a bit. There is a chance to restore peace in the South soon.

Take the Sri Lankan government, led by President Mahindra Rajapaksa, for example, which successfully suppressed the leader of the Tiger rebels in 2009 by killing Weluphilai Prabhakaran and his 24-year-old son Sared Anthony, ending a 25-year-long conflict that claimed more than 60,000 lives, nearly the same number as the 60,000 who died in southern Thailand.

Up to this day, the Thai government can take the same taunts as the leaders of Sri Lanka. Sri Lanka has to deal with the group of people who have killed and caused suffering over and over again without thinking of turning back to being good people. They just continue to cause trouble and create suffering without stopping. Society, the government and various organizations have given them opportunities and always forgiven the wrongdoers. In other words, they have given them opportunities. Turn back to being good people and not doing evil anymore. For the group of people who do not feel guilty, when the government turns around, they continue to do evil and cause trouble to each other. These groups of people must The project "Bring People Home" of the Internal Security Operations Command or ISOC Region 4, which the government proposed to jointly develop the hometown, is considered a good choice.

6
Put out the fire under the fire

We Thais must learn and recognize the necessary and sufficient behaviors and behaviors. Readers, try to look at the challenges to state power in the 3 border provinces. Under the changes in Thai society throughout the country, who would not accept that everything has changed and nothing is permanent, as the Buddha taught us, including Thai society and the world society, which are in a state of changing and being pushed. Pushing forward to follow the world's international society, there are various changes all the time from various civilizations, especially Western civilization, which has both positive and negative effects on our Thai society.

Things that have been followed, which have created a dynamic, created thoughts and Imitate, meaning imitate, learn the way of life. Foreign lifestyles have occurred so rapidly that it is difficult to stop or control. It is a change of dynamic society and civilization that is immediate. It is a factor that has resulted in the original basic civilization of Thai traditions and most Thai societies almost being gone and are about to disappear from our society.

On the contrary, research and development in technology are progressing slowly because our economy is not on par with other countries. We lack the capital and money to promote technology development as fast as the West, so it is not consistent with the import of Western technology. We are full of cities that lack research or are not very accepting of research and invention. We only dream of setting measures. And the luxurious standard of living. Trying to create a face and lifestyle that is on par with Westerners Becomes a trend of copying and imitating, which in some ways creates too much value In a disgusting and regrettable way.

The important resolution is to spread the good traditions, culture, and customs of the Thai people. Developed loosely, it lacks a clear goal. Different people, different groups, do it according to their own strengths. Each person who lacks strength lacks their own identity and is a slave to Copying other people's cultures, such as dressing provocatively, showing breasts, showing legs, showing body, and provoking emotions with those who see it horrifying and disgusting to oneself, but lacking shame, selling oneself, eating daily, like hamburgers, Italian food (Pizza), etc., instead of adjusting developing Thai food, which is the best food, making the healthiest in the world.

"Intarakiat Rodpradit," a co-author, talked about Thai food in Portland, Oregon, The United States of America, in his book "Two Friends on the American Land Adventure: My 90-Day Life Experience," is interesting. He mentioned that According to statistics, the Thai population in Portland is only 1,757 people, but there are 137 Thai restaurants. Think of it logically. Investing in a Thai restaurant in Portland will only lead to failure. But the truth is, On the contrary, Thai restaurants are making a lot of money and are on the rise. This shows that Americans and other foreigners living in Portland are increasingly consuming Thai food, while we Thais are dreaming of foreign food, which is an economic glut.

Most of our Thai society has a night market, but we try to position ourselves to be on par with Westerners, using examples as a daily fashion, such as making dogs sit like humans, making monkeys know how to dress, thinking about it is so embarrassing and shameful to our country that we Thais have forgotten who we are, where we come from, and our ancestors are Who is the world trend? Culture The popularity of the modern world has become a wave that has hit the side of Thai traditions to slow down It will end day by day, which is very regrettable. The management that is a model leader in creating local power, such as the local areas in the 3 southern border provinces, has not yet occurred with the South.

What happened, in general, was a specific earth power, specifically named "Thaksin," Which was a booming period for a while, a period of popularity of "giving for free" or finding ways to give things to "tempt," giving gifts and rewards to grassroots masses throughout the country Especially in the Northeast, "Thaksin" was particularly interested in the results The special rewards for finding one's voice in the next era are repetitive, connected to the creation of an image to warm up, so it is only superficial, not controlled, including the approval of a budget, both directly and indirectly, in the amount of a huge amount of money without any reason.

For what? In return, in response to some "popularities" for the benefit of the people, as mentioned above, for the sake of the party, which lacks conscience, lacks ethics, and lacks self-restraint. This goes against the idea of promoting community participation and self-reliance by copying past leaders, such as joint programs that are not consistent with what the people in the community want. The region, especially the southern border provinces, which have a hot problem, has Daily killings and a lot of property loss, known worldwide, as explained in the beginning. Other problems related to the southern violence And there are also other problems related to it, such as the allocation of land for people to eat. It should not be complicated. The Cabinet should not have so many decisions in each ministry, including the land-related ministries such as the Royal Property Department, the Finance Ministry, the Land Ministry, and the Agriculture and Cooperatives Ministry.

There was difficulty in issuing title deeds for making a living such the Forestry Department (at that time), including problems regarding the extent of land that the state wanted to reserve, which the writer saw as a major problem in the area, especially for making a living in 3-5 southern provinces, which caused problems in the distribution of land to the people unfairly, caused discrimination among Thai Muslims, and caused unemployment accordingly Leading to crossing the border.

Crossing the border for what? To find work in a neighboring country To bring higher income to support poor families No work, no regular income in Thailand which is an economic problem Problems of living, daily problems To survive each day and It is a specific problem of someone Of the Thai Muslims who are in hardship Poor who hold on to the assumption that the unemployed Thai Muslims must go to work in Malaysia and then earn money for many years One hundred million baht is probably true because the Malaysian dollar is worth 7 times more than the Thai dollar, which is 1 Malaysian dollar is equal to 7 baht. The chance that he will earn more than working in Thailand is actually another help to the Thai government's economy.

Therefore, Thai Muslims crossing the border as dual nationalities is a normal thing for survival. It is an understanding that has been practiced for a long time since the era when Malaysia had just gained independence from the British. There was the first leader of the Malays named Atuanku Abdul Rahman. This leader used to be a student at Wat Thepsirin Secondary School and was very close. Close to the former Thai Prime Minister at that time, Field Marshal P. Pibulsongkram, this Malaysian Prime Minister was affiliated with the UMNO party. He wanted to gain more support in the state because he was afraid of overthrow. The political authorities gave the opposition party, PASS Party, so they asked Thai Muslims in the 3 southern border provinces to register as Malays in the state of Kelantan to have the right to vote in support of the UMNO government party.

Two approaches and two nationalities, thus becoming a burden for Thailand, which currently has a population of about one hundred thousand people. Two incidents: Nationality is an old issue because it is a matter that has been neglected by the political authorities. Thai officials have ignored these problems for so long that they have become a normal issue that seems like they are not illegal but have become the "root" of the problems in the South. This issue shows the lack of understanding among local people. Very little has been reported to the central government. What about the part that is aware of the problems? As the officials are Indifferent or "indifferent," they let it solve their own problems according to their karma in every era.

The image of Muslims is seen as a group that breaks the rules of Thailand. In fact, this is the responsibility of the Immigration Bureau (Immigration Bureau) that is responsible for solving this problem in the early stages. But they were ignored because they had a part in the benefit and loss of their Thai Muslim brothers and sisters. One of the suspects in the bombing at Ratchaprasong Intersection on August 17, 2015, told the police that he was able to enter Thailand after paying the immigration police officers $600.

Financial corruption has become more important than one's own duties and the country's laws. As a result, Thai Muslims are villains of the country and are villains of the country because they are branded as "rulebreakers." No government agency is working on psychological warfare for the Thai people. Local Muslims can "reclaim their nationality." The ideology is that Thais must not allow politicians and government officials to see and sympathize with us. It is still possible to reach a time when Thai Muslim students volunteered to study in schools in Malaysia with relatively free education, citing the reason that schools and education in Thailand were forced to study the same as the standard Buddhist curriculum in Thailand, including the need to dress according to tradition, the details, and the integration of knowledge and culture. Culture must be in a balanced manner and accepted by the local people (Localization) There is no clear boundary that is consistent with the real area.

Surveying for Title Deeds in the Land Reform Area for Agriculture When the author was young, he visited his relatives in the middle of a forest that was very cold and dark. It was a place that was a state reserve in Pattani Province. He could not give details for fear that it would affect the beneficiaries. While staying with his relatives in the middle of the forest, he felt that he was in the Himalayas in the Buddhist era because it was a dark forest that made it cold. Arranged with monkeys, gibbons, and crying gibbons

In the early morning, the writer likes this kind of atmosphere very much. The fruits and roots are plentiful, as Luang Wichitwatakarn described that the Tai Yai city is plentiful. The land is good and abundant. There are large sataw trees full of sataw fruits. There are many longan, eggplant, mangoes, and mangosteens that do not belong to anyone because they are in the forest. The writer picks them and eats them as desired.

The inhabitants of this dense forest are happy with natural plants, enough, no need to buy from others. However, the influential person does not want to mention his name. He is called the boss, meaning a rich man, an elder or a person with power and influence. He ordered his employees to cut down many tall trees and sell them on the market. He claimed that he cut down trees, and he claimed that he cut down roads for people in his forest village. This residence is convenient for travel.

Of course, he has the power to destroy the forest because there are officials. The Forest Department has the share of gains and losses. There is a share of knowledge and agreement to share the benefits among themselves. Even if someone touches him, he has the power of the officials involved.

That was an event more than 50 years ago, but today, it is still the case. We cannot eliminate the dark powers that destroy the national forest reserves. Unless the officials in this new government take action according to the law, without fear of dark powers, the national forest reserves may survive. Leave some for our children and grandchildren in the future.

This is the Green era, so Go for Green. We must respect and love nature. Nature will destroy us if we do not respect and love nature. For example, there will be forest fires in the jungle. A tsunami will occur in the ocean if humans destroy the ocean, such as the oil wells under the ocean, etc. The fact is that the officials who play the game do not issue land title deeds to the owners and those who are using them. Before the date the Land Code came into force, the problem of land The ideology that creates itself by citing various reasons only creates dissatisfaction and hatred towards government officials.

When the author was sent to conduct research on minority groups by the Canadian government's funding, while the author was in the field conducting research in 3 southern border provinces, there were local Thai Muslim brothers and sisters who came to ask for negotiations with "owners."

The owner is short for "the guardian." They are equal to the governor, who takes care of the people in the community. The people in the community have the absolute right to decide to issue the title deed to the owner. And do good because they have requested it. But, the children of the owner do not Distort for various reasons because they want money from the person who asked for the title deed. It is not a fee but money under the table, which is the head of corruption. That is quite a lot of money. Where will the Thai Muslim brothers and sisters get the money to pay under the table to the officials? Even the land title deed fee is already very difficult. Their lives are hard to live from morning to night. Americans call them. These people say that From check to check because they are very poor. They do not have the knowledge or ability to contact to get the land title deed. They do not even know the initial process. They are also afraid of the officials who threaten them and use impolite words, such as saying that "he speaks the Indian language," meaning the Jawi language.

These words made Muslim brothers and sisters feel inferior. Some of them even turned their backs and asked the terrorists for help. When the terrorists helped, they had a condition that they would join the terrorist group. This was one of the reasons that arose from the performance of their duties. Of the government officials, which is a cause linked to the unrest in the 3 southern border provinces.

The writer has negotiated with the owner and received the answer that *"Doctor, if anything is legal and in accordance with the regulations, I will take action immediately. Just pay a fee."*

The author has used personal funds from the Canadian and American governments that supported the author's research to help hundreds of Thai Muslims to own their farmland. They are happy to have their own property to earn a living, which has made them love Thailand.

This is one dimension that can show the government the relationship that is connected to each other, which will lead to another good result and peace. The government should have a special project to exempt the fee for the poor in the rural areas so that they do not have to pay the land title fee. This will make these Thai Muslims feel good about the government and they There will be understanding and support from the government, which will also have a positive effect on governance because they agree with the government.

This is certainly a dimension of social science, anthropology and psychology that can create a solid relationship between our Thai Muslim brothers and sisters in the locality and the state.

This is what the government wants. The civil war can be easily solved. The problem of terrorism and unrest in the local society of our Thai Muslim brothers and sisters can also be solved. On the other hand, when the system cannot support the free trade area (FTA = Free Trade Area) that has not yet been passed by the parliament but the government has already agreed to sign it. We are stepping into the global system, which can have many trading partners, including 8 countries and 1 group country.

But unfortunately, there are still many problems in Thailand. They are problems that cannot be solved. When we cannot solve our internal problems, how can we join other countries in an international way or FTA? We should solve our own internal problems first, especially in the 3 southern border provinces of Thailand. If we can solve the FTA problems, other problems will be easier to solve. And the goal will be achieved according to the intention of the country's leader. Stop talking, stop advertising, and persuade. It's a lie. Let it be the politician's job. Government officials must do their duty honestly and honestly. The people of the whole nation will be able to look back at you once again. We must put the FTA on hold and turn to solve domestic problems that still have many challenges and reaffirm our successes in advance.

The author has worked with the Laem Son camp soldiers and village headmen to request them not to destroy the forest. They obeyed very well. The author has worked with the Department of Public Welfare, the military, and local leaders during the research in the field in both the North and the South and has been successful in requesting them not to burn the forest. However, the dark forces have invaded and destroyed the forest in many regions throughout Thailand, including 3 southern border provinces of Thailand.

They agreed to stop the destruction of forests because they agreed with the benefits of the whole country. But later, the conflict became more severe because of the competition for resources by taking advantage of the loopholes in the law. Even politicians were supporting them. Even at the military level, if the state did not support the support, it would not be possible.

Solve the southern problem well and appropriately. When the American leader is killed in the war, the leader will express condolences and mourn the families of the soldiers who died. But the Thai leader, Thaksin, attacked with the sentence, that Serves you right. While the southern bandits robbed the gun, instead of expressing condolences to his family as they served the country in defending the country, did not support and also spoke sarcastically, that, "Serves you right," which a leader of the country should not do. It is more pathetic and embarrassing to the world that Thailand has a bad leader like Thaksin.

In Taksin's view, the military acts as mere subordinates and slaves because they only earn the country's salary or because those in power in the country like to protect and support capitalists to use as political capital for campaigning, both in terms of building tourist resorts, in order to build prestige and increase their own power, and they cannot help but hide their own personal benefits, such as being suspicious of the use of national budget in a hidden manner. Creating popularity in the party, especially by setting aside a huge budget as a "central budget," which the powerful can order to spend without limits, which is the origin of legitimate corruption. If we cannot eliminate the behavior of politicians at the leading level to feel afraid of injustice, it will only create a loss of trust from the people, making it difficult to achieve benefits.

7
Let's review and talk about the problem The unrest in the South

The leadership status, originally from the 4th Army, had absolute power through the Internal Security Organization (domestic) that gave the power to transfer, reward, and remunerate. This absolute power must be in the complete Ten Royal Virtues and must have "Leadership" to be classified in the category of Ten Royal Virtues in the deep and profound meaning that "We govern Land by Dharma." In addition to the youth, there are also many elderly people in the 3 southern border provinces. On average, they are unemployed. Some of them live in "Ponoh" schools, almost losing their enthusiasm.

But for the youth and the youth with an average age of 30, it occurs in large numbers. This is because birth control cannot be performed according to customs and traditions. What are the causes of men having multiple wives? The reason is that the government does not provide knowledge and enforce public health measures. They cannot provide birth control or abortion as in the modern world. The custom of men having up to 4 wives or more is the main factor that causes children to be more followed, causing the problem of overpopulation.

While China and India are trying to pass laws to protect Muslims, the number of children, families, and populations is increasing, and some families are "poor," struggling with finances, lacking appropriate clothing, and lacking money to buy medicines to maintain health. The poverty of Muslim brothers and sisters in this area has increased quite a lot. This is a youth problem every year. Because they were abandoned, left to live as they please. Anyone can have sex. Anyone can have children, even dogs. They can do it without having to take responsibility for the children that are born. But the responsibility is without the babies that are born blaming the government for not helping with the problem. There are only people who complain and criticize the government.

The truth is that the reason why I made myself poor is because I don't want to work, but I tend to Be obsessed with the things in my head, so the problems follow, as if the youth were abandoned. The warmth and lack of a proper way of life that will be sufficient, so they lived in the original Pondok, which was a place of shelter by chance, but the Pondok had "Tor Khru" as the owner, which is like the abbot of a Buddhist temple, the leader of the ashram, the house, the overnight stay, which has a religious leader who is called a pondok school. Therefore, the youths learned about the cultural network, the culture of Learning from within your own heart amidst the raging trend of consumer culture. What is the main goal that must still be maintained? ... Religious principles Because religion will help develop the minds of children and youth of the next generation. From us, they grow up every day. Therefore, we must rely on youth who have been trained by the teacher's desk. This is the doctrine taken seriously in Muslim society in the 3 southern border provinces.

General youth problems in the 3 southern border provinces

There are many young Muslims in Thailand who are growing up to be human beings and do not have to live like ordinary humans. Many of these young people are "unemployed," which is the cause of poverty. Some of them are good at seeking knowledge and have abilities; about 5-10% who dream of studying abroad want to seek funds to study abroad, increasing the number of countries that have reached their goal. For example, in Egypt, there are about 2,000 Thai students studying abroad and in other countries, a large number of them.

The author believes that the government should take care of this issue and the government should provide support by providing educational scholarships instead of allowing foreigners to lend their hands without control. It must be acknowledged that there are both domestic and international processes that want to lend these scholarships to young people to study by making a contract in advance. When they return to Thailand, they will automatically be easily involved in the process. It is a social contract that binds both legally and religiously and cannot be violated.

This is one of the results that is an opportunity for the youth to participate in creating unrest in the 3 southern border provinces. But if the government provides further assistance in terms of educational scholarships, it will be able to take care of them all and will be of great benefit to the stability and economy of the society of our southern people.

Which terrorist groups should we be concerned about?

When we understand the youth behavior movement, it makes us think back to this group of youth and the group that is very worrisome and dangerous in the society of the 3 southern border provinces of Thailand because it is a united front or in English called "United Front" that can turn back the sense of division of the land in the 3 southern border provinces. Southern provinces in the past have actually existed. The government must take action to "defeat this idea without fighting" to lose both the government and the United Front. This is the first thing that the government must do immediately by reaching out to develop and improve with the principle of "psychological warfare."

Youth were unemployed, the government could not create jobs for them, and the land division of agriculture is called "overall failure." some went to find jobs in neighboring countries such as Malaysia and Singapore, some go to Indonesia according to their own wishes, they think that the Thai government has abandoned them, abandoned their people, they must turn to rely on neighboring countries in order to

"Help yourself" Being a dual nationality should be right, including the politicians' ultimatum for personal gain and the negligence for decades.

The wrongs that have been committed have become normal, ordinary becomes a matter that is treated as a matter of conduct, while the legal matter has not yet had time to start to be corrected. The unrest, the weakening of the administration, the suppression that is still today, and the new government, when reading the recommendations of this Government Handbook, must be awakened. Accelerate development to reach and solve problems immediately. This problem will end. Peace in the 3 southern border provinces will return.

Ransom

Ransom is common worldwide, including in the United States. However, in the three southern border provinces, ransom was started by rubber cutters. The more rubber they extract, the more they pay. The rubber plantation owners also collect the tax. Otherwise, it is not safe. This point, in addition to The state does not support agricultural land, which is a public area. The state reserves it for no use, so it is encroached on without any cause. Doing anything seriously

Rubber species are also similar, lacking quality. Even if they were available, they would not reach the local people. However, the government (especially during the Thaksin era) promoted other regions to send good rubber species to the Northeast. When the author visited Sisaket Province, he was proud that the farmers in Sisaket had good rubber species to plant and benefited from the extraction of good quality rubber. The price of rubber in the market is higher than that of the three southern border provinces. This is because rubber farmers in the 3 southern border provinces have low-quality rubber varieties, and the farther they are, the less opportunity they have to receive assistance, etc.

"It is unfair" and the choice of corrective action must be made immediately In order for the local people to see "fairness" and not just a one-time correction but must be done continuously no matter which government it is.

Study

Returning to the dimensions of education in the three southern border provinces, it is believed that both the readers and the writers will agree that there is a lack of care from the state or that care is not thorough and not thorough and not willing. The state must use school management as a base to build strength by using personnel who have the intelligence, the spirit, and the leadership, like Khru Pipat Dumdeang, who sacrificed his own monthly income to develop the school by buying more land to build a school building because the number of students increased. He also built a library so that people who were away from home could read newspapers. and search for knowledge to be the center of the community, cutting the road to make it more convenient for local people to travel and visit each other. Find funds to help students who are good at studying. Please see the history of Khru Phiphat Dumdeang.

The author used to think that he was a person who liked to sacrifice. However, if compared with the sacrifice of Khru Pipat Dumdeang, the author's older brother, then it is not comparable at all. In addition to being a teacher with high ideals, Khru Pipat is also a person who has great sacrifice, sacrificing even his life and dedicating himself to society and others all along.

General San Chitpatima, Chief of Staff, Surasak Son Suea and senior officers of Pattani Province changed the name of the school from "Kubo" School, where Khru Pipat Dumdeang taught and improved until it was accepted by the government and the public, to "Phatthan Suksa" School as a memorial to Khru Pipat because of the work he had done for this locality. This society and the country's Nation.

Kru Pipat has a high level of leadership and relies on cooperation. He is a leader who is an important person together with other parties such as service strategy, teachers, and parents (most parents, 99.09%, are Muslims). Kru Pipat understands and reaches out to the Thai Muslim people in the area clearly. They fully believe in the honesty of Khru Pipat. The local leaders and the community give freedom to make decisions and determine the "balance" that creates teachers who are sufficient and develop students to their full potential according to each person's potential to be the real center, not fake. In addition, the sense of love must be integrated. Compassion, Gratitude Gratitude to the homeland in the 3 southern border provinces and throughout Thailand.

Society

"Ta Dee Ka" Society "Ponor" The state must find a way to help make the image appear to reflect the reality outside the classroom.

Language

Thai is the national language of the whole country. It is a tool for communication and knowledge-seeking. The teaching curriculum must be effective. Thai language teaching must be given top priority. Good students in the Thai language category will receive special gifts as encouragement. It will make them see the importance of the Thai language in their future in their lives. Strategies to use the language as a mother language harmoniously and make it an important mother language. Ranked number one among the three southern border provinces.

Establishment of a Center for Higher Education Institutions

Creating the best complete higher education center in Southeast Asia will be the most important part. "It is a problem of conditions" even though it takes time to teach up to the doctoral or doctoral level. Preparing the budget, personnel, and location is a clear strategy to bring people from all sectors into the area. It is a clear creation of the future. It is harder to refuse than personnel from other regions, such as the Northeast, who settled in the South. In one era, there were many Thai Muslim brothers and sisters who converted from Thai Buddhists to Muslims in the area.

When the author was conducting research in the southern border provinces, he interviewed them in the Lao language to gain a good understanding of their background. However, the government's development approach did not yield significant results. It must cooperate with the religious and cultural dimensions of "local areas" in order to maintain ideological diversity. This is still part of the youth's existence. It must be done from the early teenage years.

Ministry of Education

The Ministry of Education's duty is to accept the differences in many rules and original concepts in the Thai Education Act. It is necessary for the government to adjust them to be appropriate for the time and place.

Even in America, there are special exceptions for the poor blacks and Indians (in some areas) because they are still very backward and behind in education. America can improve for the minorities. We, Thailand, should be able to do it, too. We have many academics who graduated from the United States. We must come and help improve our country, Thailand. No matter which region, the South or other regions

Of course, the 3 southern border provinces have urgent needs that the government must develop. Education is the basic standard and must be continuous, not just doing it stoppingly. It cannot be effective if it is not done continuously. Use the school director as a coordinator, such as Khru Phiphat Dumdeang, the author's brother, who has practiced by being a resource person to provide knowledge and training. To teachers and government administrators to understand the concept between schools and families and communities to create common goals and help develop children and youths to have quality in the future, to have a standard of life (Life Standard) along with creating a sense of gratitude to the land, helping poor youths with kindness and with warmth, compassion and kindness consistently and adjusting themselves.

This is how we can say with full confidence that "Students are the center" (Student Center) in America. There is a building for students to express their own freedom of thought called the Sub-Student Union Building. In Thailand, we can do the same and should do it, especially in the 3 southern border provinces, to be a place for students to express themselves and keep up with the modern world in the 21st century.

Stability

The military institution, which was the main institution, has been weakened, especially in the fieldwork. The ideology of the military leader has become increasingly tied to Thai politicians, especially the Prime Minister. It lacks the solidarity, the rank, and the dignity of being a true soldier. The strength in the ethics and culture of the original organization. The structure of the military that is on the way or that is sluggish should be corrected. Became different people because they believed that each person had power and was respectful of the military leaders, like (kissing or kissing the boss. The institution does not teach to be a "thinker" but teaches to listen to the commander with discipline, which is a good thing for resisting the enemy only, but it has an impact on the stability of our country.

Who is the commander? The commander is just a boss, a supervisor, but not a life boss who dictates everything because he wants too much in return from his position, which becomes his own weak point and that of the institution. The military should be the main force of the institution of the land, with loyalty and stability in the independence and sovereignty of the nation, according to the main strategy of the nation (Grand Strategy), such as Defending and preserving the independence of the nation is a matter of the entire nation and the entire parliament (the author is grateful for the Queen's grace in stating that the southern problem is a problem of the entire nation that must be solved together, not a problem of any one person).

A declaration of a state of war or a change in strategy from accepting to an invasion is not a decision of the Cabinet but must be a decision that is … The decision of the whole nation, all military leaders must have "intelligent" knowledge and understanding and dare to take risks (Know how to take the risk) in making decisions that are full of morality and ethics of the institution and the nation.

The pursuit of strategy

Don't think that only the South and the soldiers in the South must have the condition of

The leader of the search for a strategy and the use of force must have a strategic basis.

The strategy of "principle" and use of force as a single dimension. The deployment of forces in the strategy of the South has been determined according to the geography, including the defense of the sea territory, the situation surrounding the daily attack, the intention of the procession, The skilled training of the evil people, the devils who have been trained from both in and abroad Some of them came from ISIS, which is behind world crimes including the unrest in the 3 southern border provinces.

Starting with demanding ransom for a 13-year-old girl to be sold as a slave and forced to become a wife themselves, changing the teachings of Allah to be their own teachings by referring to the true religion to be a fake religion, teaching them to hate the Western world's traditions and those who follow the civilizational ideology The West, especially America (ISIS), has set a base of hatred, etc.

Fighters in various movements with ideologies fleeing to foreign countries, dangers and disasters from the actions of corrupt officials who use the bureaucratic apparatus to make a living on the backs of Muslims and Thais, which are many times more than the ideological groups at every level and every sect, instead of solving the problem quickly, they intend to keep the problem in order to Political and financial interests, monopoly businesses in the area

Both legal and illegal, even the killing of innocent people, monks, slander, scapegoating and slandering each other in a blanket may lead to the collapse of the nation in this era. If this government does not understand the people of the government and Muslims in every inch of detail, our country will be in a state of disaster. Every day and every night, in the end, it will be too difficult or too late to fix.

The author would like to ask the government whether those in power can distinguish between who will solve the problem… and who is the problem creator… Death such as the death of Khru Pipat Dumdeang and other victims of murder, both in the past and present, who caused it? Who is behind the spider web?

Mixed with the story in each case and allowed to float freely in the society near the center of power, there are people who are taken to be victims in the power game, such as Muslims in the area, including lawyer Somchai Neelapaijit, plus the daily killing of suspects in the case of Mr. Somchai, etc., is a good example of the unrest or what is called "smoke under the fire."

Finally, the charges of police and government corruption will be cleared because they are blinded by greed for money or dollars (as Americans say). The case of the arrest of the killer of Khru Pipat Dumdeang is a prime example of evidence that shows that government officials have committed the most shameful misconduct by using their positions to seek personal benefits.

The evidence that is The suspect is the gun in question, which is registered in the name of Khru Phiphat Dumdeang. The suspect, after killing Khru Phiphat, took the gun in question with him. The important evidence is that the gun of the deceased was in the possession of the suspect and was arrested. This became insufficient evidence to order a lawsuit. This is because the officers, The police who handled the case, together with the prosecutor at that time, ordered not to prosecute the case.

The author investigated the reason why the prosecutor did not sue, which was because of bribing the defendant in the amount of millions of baht. At that time, it was considered quite a lot. The first case owner had a second-hand Honda car. But after the case of Khru Pipat Dumdeang and Mr. Kiang Chantrat, it turned out that the related officers had a new Benz car that was used in a flash, causing damage to the government sector. They did not maintain their morals. The dignity of being a justice officer is not even a little bit.

Even though the whole city knows well that the evidence is the gun that the perpetrators own is the gun of Khru Pipat Dumdeang. They have successfully killed according to their plan and seized the gun to destroy and kill others next. There are people who are taken as victims of power. For example, the Muslims in the area, including Mr. Somchai Neelapaijit, as mentioned earlier, if the problem is left unresolved, the situation will escalate to a conflict between our Thai Muslim brothers and sisters and the Thai government.

Islam

Islam is a religion of ideology and the struggle of Islam. It has set a universal system in itself that Muslims all over the world are brothers and sisters. There will be a group of violent Muslims who have a strong faith spirit and use death as a weapon. We must help each other to solve the problems. Help like this or lack of reason like this (Sickism Sicking, Belief of Death) because it is a danger to the South In the 3 border provinces, it is a danger to the world that we live together. There should be an improvement of the police system structure that has up to 3 command centers in the South to leave only local police that report directly to the command of the provincial governor. Change all old policies and turn to use new policies. To act promptly on the incidents of the people from the police, which the writer will call the new policy (Provincial Politician) or the provincial policy, where the governor has the right to make decisions alone and supports the 3 regional commands that must have strong leadership in the integrated system with the law as the foundation and the law as the support.

Justice Process

When it comes to the justice process and the true decentralized power according to Article 78 of the Constitution of the Kingdom of Thailand B.E. 2540, let's look at the soldiers who are in the middle in order to help the public move forward to destroy the roots of the degenerate society automatically.

Let's see and observe that the administration will imitate the 66/23 policy, which is a policy of suppression and targeting 3 goals, namely, having a party, forces and allies, and then will receive initial success. Not only that but in terms of actual practice, the 66/23 policy order is a democracy policy that is not yet complete. The announcement of the Attorney General's Law from the 4th Army Region under the green light from the government.

Therefore, the cancellation is good if it is carried out to the level of "safety" without interference from politicians, including both inside and outside the country. It is appropriate in the behavior and behavior that is necessary and sufficient to bring "peace" back to the 3 southern border provinces of Thailand.

8
Vicious Cycle
In the 3 Southern Border Provinces

One of the most difficult southern border wars in the world to resolve was the long-running conflict between the Pulo rebels and their networks, including the BRN movement, and the Thai government, which began in 1902, when the Thai government (then Siam) took control of Pattani. The Pattani rulers were brought in. The last king of Pattani, named Tengku Abdul Kader Kamaruddin, came to Bangkok.

The purpose was to force Tengku to record his signature in agreement with the King of Siam's wishes. However, Tengku insisted on upholding the sovereignty of Pattani. In the end, he was sent to Phitsanulok along with some others, who even died in Phitsanulok. However, he was later pardoned and ordered to return to Pattani, but he decided to seek refuge in Kantang until the end. His Majesty was born there in the year 2476.

In the year 2445, it was the year that Pattani lost its power to Siam, which was the loss of sovereignty of the various rulers and the people of Pattani. The rights, freedom and independence were under the power of the King of Siam. The death of Tengku Abdul Kader Kamaruddin, the King of Pattani, was the end of the Pattani monarchy. And was the fuse that started the hatred towards the land of Siam ever since. There were more than 5,500 deaths.

Especially in 2004, during the Thaksin government, many people lost their lives, and the number of conflicts increased exponentially. No sign of it. The way to end it is similar to the Shadow War. These rebel groups are jointly pursuing "independence" according to the original goal.

But will gain some "self-governance" in Southeast Asia (SEA), including Sri Lanka (Little Tiger – Tamil, Singapore), Indonesia, Philippines, etc. Especially in the southern part of Thailand, it is a war of conflict And has become a "southern fire" that is raging every day. Today, it is not only frightening or affecting only Thailand, but also neighboring countries and the whole world. The suffering of the South is not only suffering in Thailand but also in many countries around the world.

The root truth of the suffering, broadly speaking, and the Malay Muslims want Thai people to confirm and elevate their status to be "Muslim Malay" to as high as possible, not wanting the state to look down on them again. One purpose is to have the state look at them as they were originally, according to their history of living before Thai rule.

That is to say, to have his own sultan, he has his own freedom, without anyone interfering with him. This is the cycle of madness of the Malay Muslims. Some groups that are fighting against the state, such as the BRN, will be mad in any way, in the form of human dignity, without killing both their own people and the Buddhists, especially the Malay Muslims. And pure Buddhists, such as children, women, monks, teachers, nurses, doctors, businessmen, fishermen, farmers, rice farmers, gardeners, and people who are not involved in their madness.

These people did not interrupt the madness of the crazy dance. In his eyes, politics is a vicious and evil act that is done day after day, repeated over and over again. It is the cycle of the rebels, like mad dogs. This is called the cycle of evil.

Therefore, the vicious cycle must be stopped and ended now, just like the Thai government that killed innocent Muslims, citing unfair reasons and creating unnecessary stories to eliminate the government, such as the case of lawyer Somchai Nilapai Chit, who gave his opinion that using the vicious cycle is wrong. Or violate human rights. Thaksin knew well that Somchai might be the core of the Malay Muslim society that would stop The injustice of Thailand caused him to be ordered to be killed, which followed the prophetic pattern of the leader, Haji Sulong, in 2500.

This repeated incident is the vicious cycle of the Thai government. If Thais do not know the word human dignity or human rights, then they must stop creating evil in the land of Siam any longer. Find a way to achieve peace to be worthy of the word "Siam, the land of smiles," which is a country that is cheerful and free. In fact, the local people are both Thai and Muslim. Especially people in the village, Villagers, people from the countryside, people from the city, people living in remote areas and those who are concerned. In the case of following the unrest in the southern part of Thailand

The author himself, who has been following for a long time, believes and is confident that both the government and the rebel groups, all groups, will find it difficult to defeat each other with military force because no matter how they fight, they will still be fighting each other. The battle lines between the two sides have barely progressed. But the reason for continuing to fight each other is to seize the opportunity. Compare the battlefield as much as possible. For what? Or to use the power to negotiate. In what negotiations? Negotiating the same thing over and over again. This, the author will call the "Cycle of Viciousness." It has been going on for decades and must continue to be so as long as the "politics" of both sides are not serious and sincere in creating permanent peace and never take the promises.

Words are of little value, and actions are of high value. We must rely on strong leaders from both the state and the process, keep their word, say what and do it, and not talk in a way that puts people in front and dogs behind their backs, which is like negotiating every day. Today, it is a game of politicians who play to show off to the people and make the world crazy that they will solve the problems in the South.

The word "to solve the problem" is not applicable. It must be solved and solved at the right point. The fire under Even if it can be put out because waiting for the day to pass, more people will die. Look back and see within 8 years, the statistics of the fire under 5,469 people have died. The trend of causing incidents will increase Or decrease in any way. The author has researched, recorded, and summarized as follows.

As a writer, I would like to use the appropriate term that is consistent with the current situation, which is the term "Cycle of Ugliness." Why does the writer call it the Cycle of Uglyness? Because the conflict between the two sides has dragged on for centuries and will never end. The government is raising a gang of thieves and terrorists. At the same time, The terrorist movement also feeds the government, and the terrorist movement also feeds war because they want the national budget.

The government currently allocates the national budget for this program since the budget giver and the budget recipient have tax money from the people. Thai people spend money wisely as the incident has been happening for a long time. It is believed that if the Border Patrol Police (BPP) go on patrol at any time, at any point, they must inform the terrorist group (KJK). If the terrorist group wants to sabotage, burn down a school, etc., they will tell the police. The Border Patrol found out about this incident. The newspaper said that the perpetrator had already fled without knowing the name.

This is how we can trust and have confidence in the government. The government raises war. War is a great resort and a source of income for the political budget and the military. As long as the government really takes the lasting peace and happiness to the south, what will be the end (summary)? What will happen?

Put out the fire in the South by solving the problems behind the unrest on the southern border of Thailand.

When the author returned to visit his hometown in early 1976 after the death of his eldest brother, Khru Pipat Dumdeang, on June 25, 1976, at 2:30 p.m., nearly 40 years ago, the author wanted to write about the causes and reasons behind the author's writing of this story, which occurred 10 years ago while he was staying at the farm. The writer's book Read every issue, some daily, some weekly, there will be both new and old issues. Review what happened to 3 provinces plus 4 districts in the southern part of Thailand. The writer read only the headlines and felt his heart drop, and he felt sad. It is indescribable and cannot be described in perfect language from the feeling that he intended to know what happened in his hometown, our sleeping city Which is becoming a barren, uncivilized forest town every day now.

Why? There are more and more evil people who think badly of the country. Has the government made such a serious mistake in taking care of our southern country that the Southerners should not be forgiven? This is an important question that the writer is very interested in. The writer's original thought, now that we are talking about different things, we must also talk about similarities. Let's look at whether the government cares or not. In terms of conflict, the government has not given up on solving problems, no matter how difficult they are. However, sometimes the government acts in an autonomous manner, such as during the Thaksin government, which only used personal influence because it believed that the problems in the South were caused by "petty thieves," such as the destruction of the Ponoh. In fact, the government should operate in accordance with the royal initiative of His Majesty the King, which is "understand, reach, develop" as the main principle for solving problems in every region. Which will allow for a fairly large number of problem-solving.

The opposite is true.

Behind the unrest in the southern border of Thailand We must spend time studying and researching in detail the problems of unrest in the South. The problem of conflict in the southern border provinces of Thailand is a very complicated problem. There are many causes. Much of the information is described at the beginning. Let me emphasize again. The causes of the problem are both racial conflicts. And Religion The southern border provinces of Thailand used to be the land of Hindus and Buddhists. In the past, according to the development of the cycle of life, Islam has become more and more important. Malay Muslims are more and more. It is a multiplication, and the government of this place has been changed to a sultanate system. Of Pattani the name of the city is "Patining" or "Pattani".

Later, Siam became stronger politically, administratively, economically, military-wise, and so on, and had influence over this region for more than 700 years. During the European colonial period, Siam had to cede some southern territories to the United Kingdom in 1909. This area was divided into two parts (two areas), one of which was annexed. Together with the British Territory, and later became part of Malaysia, the other part remained in Siam, which is now Thailand.

Comments and recommendations for the State Review "1" "2"

If we think in detail in terms of history, the colonization of European emperors, etc., India and Burma have been unified, and Malaysia, too, by England, Cambodia, and Vietnam, have been unified by France, and the Philippines has been unified by the United States.

Why? We, Thais, have not liberated the unity of the "Kingdom of Pattani." We have lost nothing since we cannot keep them. We have only lost the blood of thousands of Thais. These unfortunate people, including the writer's brother, fought for Thailand, for the motherland, and for what we are aiming for. What do Muslims want? Has the government come to ask themselves? Do they want to take their land back? Because we have taken it and robbed it since the Ayutthaya period, 1767. Since the Ayutthaya period, we have had problems with Muslims. We have sacrificed a lot of blood, life, things, buildings, houses, and spaces. More soldiers died on this land than American soldiers died in the Iraq War or the Middle East War.

When it comes to differences, we must also talk about similarities. When I was a theology teacher at Washington University, I found not only similarities and similarities between religions but also differences. Therefore, I believe that differences are one and the same.

Isn't the government oppressing the southern people too much?

Yes, if the government does not give freedom, the belief of the people of the South, especially Muslims, of course, the government oppresses them because it is not consistent with the word democracy. In the case of the conflict that occurred in the South, peace has been replaced by "violence." Hundreds of thousands of lives have been lost, including the life of one of the writer's brothers, and there are also many injured. It is difficult to get the exact numbers. Children, villagers, gardeners, and innocent people are also included in the net, including monks and babies.

Of course... The government's proposal for economic development in the South is currently another measure that is in the right direction. However, the writer's idea, trying to solve the conflict through development and reconciliation is part of the right thing. Why?

Because the root of the southern problem is not development or The reconciliation between the two nationalities, Thai and Malaysian, as Dr. Wan Kadir Jehman has given an idea which is contrary to the opinion of the writer, is that the problem mostly arises from the fact that Malay-Muslims are separated and treated as "subjects of internal colonial rule," which is that they are given less justice. Or as a foster child or Second-class

Are the rights to hold religion and practice customs, traditions and culture restricted to the point of feeling oppressed? In fact, King Rama VI warned the government to give freedom and respect for the customs and culture of Muslims in this land, which is clearly evident in the royal initiatives of King Rama VI. The question is, why doesn't the government try to apply it to the Muslims at present?

Let's look at the Thai people in the southern region.

What do Thais who are Buddhists think? What is wrong with them? Why are they always being killed and destroyed? Is it normal for Thais to be killed continuously by the Muslim opposing side? Or is it normal for the state? Or does the state think that the dead are not the flesh and blood of the state, so it lets the matter pass without paying attention or making it a serious matter? What is so hot when the government is living happily, having power, having good cars, having huge bank deposits, having both small and big wives happily, having a lot of influence, using rhetoric to deceive, brainwash uneducated people and following not being aware of various tricks or using money power to buy people to be on their side of themselves, speaking things without sincerity like people who speak in front and put dogs behind their backs

Murder is a problem of the Southern people, not the state. For example, when a senior figure like Thaksin said, "It's a good thing that soldiers are killed," etc., a leader who said, "Human life is human life," no matter who it is, of course, if someone is killed, bullied, oppressed, or If the child is the flesh and blood of a minister or a member of the government or the family of a person in the government, it will be immediately corrected.

Muslims, such as some who are civil servants or my brother, who has been a teacher for decades or is a government official, are they wrong to be killed so cruelly? Even though my brother has done so much for the youth without any regard or discrimination against all races and religions for decades.

He was brutally murdered by a group of bad guys without any chance to fight back. Because of the planned killing, like a pack of dogs for a single person and no chance to stand up, some dogs still know how to respect the dogs in their own group. If the dog is cornered and can't fight back, a good gangster dog will stop the cornered dog because it is a good dog, a dog that is a good gangster with morals.

But these "Muslim" villains, after committing the brutal act against the writer's brother, saw that he was not dead yet, poured gasoline on the writer's brother and burned him alive. Or Muslims who declare themselves to be fighters who adhere to the teachings of the Prophet on mercy and not harming fellow human beings

Such acts that are regularly shown to the world show that they are human beings. They have become human beings only, but their hearts are not human at all. They are hellish ghosts with only evil in their blood. They may claim to be Muslims, but their behavior is not good for Muslims.

If we Thais do this to this evil Muslim group, it will be in line with what they have done. What did you do to the writer's brother? How would a Muslim brother feel if he was a good Muslim or a true Muslim? Try to answer like a Muslim who is also a human being.

Let's see the next one, the moral, the sacred, the monks who are the symbol of our country because monks are considered pure and have no conflict with anyone, especially people of other religions. Why were they killed and beheaded so cruelly? It's as if there has been a grudge against each other for hundreds of lifetimes or hundreds of years. The monk was ordained to reduce his lust. He did not come to be involved in politics. He did not come to fight or clash with anyone. So why did you come to kill him? This is the evil, the cruelty that the Muslim group, the evil group who used religion as a front, committed in 3 provinces and 4 districts in the southern part of Thailand.

This is only part of the truth. In reality, the number of violent incidents in the three southern border provinces of Thailand is many times greater. If we take the history of terrorist incidents from the year Thaksin came to power to the year his sister became the Prime Minister of Thailand, she is pure. Both Thai Buddhists and Thai Muslims who want to make a living Honest people have to flee to live in many provinces. How pitiful it would be. So sad. Our southern region has been forgotten by the government. It is done to show or to gain face, not from sincerity.

Except during the time of Prime Minister Chuan Leekpai and Prime Minister Prem Tinsulanonda, who used the Cool South policy as a policy to solve the problems in the South effectively. The result and the subsequent time of Prime Minister Chuan Leekpai, considered it as the policy of Pa Prem. It was an effective solution to the problems in the South as well.

During the time when Prime Minister Thaksin Shinawatra was the prime minister, he was not interested in using this approach as the main principle for solving the problem. He had a narrow-minded view that the terrorist act was the work of petty thieves only. As a result, the solution to the problem resulted in a huge mistake. With Thaksin's iron law theory, there was the brutal killing of Muslims who opposed the rule in many cases.

In the case of Tak Bai, the incident occurred in October 2547, when soldiers arrested six protesters out of 2,000 protesters and took them to the Tak Bai detention center.

The November 2004 edition of the Nation newspaper described the brutality of state officials towards the protesters, which resulted in 78 deaths, saying that it would be an overstatement to mention the incident as more than the slaughter of cows and buffaloes that were heading to the slaughterhouse.

The case of the Krue Se Mosque is another case that shows the cruelty of Thaksin Shinawatra's government in solving the problem, as Oranong and Associate Professor Nakarin Mektrairat have compiled according to the opinions of Associate Professor Nariniti Setthabutra and Associate Professor Dr. Niyom Rathamrit as follows:

The incident known as the Krue Se Mosque incident was a violent incident that occurred on 28 April 2004 in the area of the old mosque in Pattani Province. The violence in the three southern border provinces of Thailand has been ongoing since the arson attack in Klong Luang, Narathiwat Ratchanakarin. On January 4, 2547, The content is summarized as follows:

On April 27, 2547, at approximately 15:00 p.m., a group of people dressed in ordinary clothing went to perform religious duties at the Krue Se Mosque, carrying their bags. When the time came, they prayed together. Usta Soh gave a speech to encourage them to be determined to declare independence and planned to steal the guns of the officers at the Krue Se checkpoint and then flee to hide in the mosque.

The insurgents attacked and clashed with the military authorities, killing three soldiers and police officers and injuring 17 others. The 32 insurgents fled to the Krue Se Mosque, where an estimated 2,000–3,000 people had gathered. The authorities cordoned off the mosque for a long time, waiting until 2:00 p.m. when Gen. Pallabh Pimanee, deputy director-general of the department, arrived. Previously, he ordered police and military officers to storm the mosque "using grenades and weapons," resulting in the deaths of all 32 insurgents inside the mosque.

The impact of the incident of the invasion of the Krue Se Mosque has spread throughout the world, causing criticism of the government's excessive brutality in the suppression.

From Kru Se to Tak Bai

The brutal crackdown on dissidents with weapons during Thaksin Shinawatra's government resulted in a huge loss of life. Just a few months after the Krue Se incident, a massacre occurred, resulting in the deaths of 85 people due to the brutality of the crackdown.

The incident occurred when six local men were arrested, and a march demanded their release. The police called for reinforcements from the army after some marchers threw rocks and tried to blockade the police station, and security officers used tear gas and fired back.

Hundreds of local people, mostly young men, were arrested, stripped of their shirts, had their hands tied behind their backs and were made to lie flat on the ground. Leaked YouTube videos showed soldiers kicking and beating people who were restrained and lying on the ground, unable to help themselves.

Later that afternoon, the arrested people were thrown into trucks by soldiers to be transported to a military camp in Pattani Province. The arrested people were piled up five or six stories high inside the trucks. When the trucks arrived at the military camp three hours later, many of the arrested people had already died of suffocation.

Media reports later reported that seven people died from gunshot wounds, while the rest were believed to have died of suffocation or were beaten.

Consequences

The incident sparked widespread dissatisfaction and protests across the country. VCDs produced by Muslim groups showed the footage of the incident, as well as the critical voices of the VCDs, which were later circulated among Muslim groups in Thailand. The government said that the possession of This VCD is illegal and states that the government can sue those who have the VCD in their possession.

Shortly after the incident, Prime Minister Thaksin Shinawatra's first reaction was that the men died because "they were still weak from fasting during the month of Ramadan."

The author and co-authors agree that Thaksin's statement was an act of self-defense, taking advantage of the time when Muslims were fasting, which led to increased resentment and a crackdown that resulted in the deaths of those whom the authorities claimed were insurgents. To die in the Krue Se Mosque, which is considered a sacred place for Muslims, is an extremely inappropriate act and an act that goes beyond what is necessary. It only caused hatred among Muslims who have The government's power and the order of General Pallabh Pinmanee to use weapons to suppress the incident. If the order or approval of the Prime Minister at that time, Thaksin Shinawatra, was not received, it would have been impossible.

The case of the transfer of Mr. Phradon Suwannarat from the Director of the Southern Border Provinces Administrative Center (SBPAC) to work in the Ministry of Interior simply because Mr. Phradon is a high-level official who has high self-esteem and works in support of the Democrat Party's policies in resolving conflicts in the three southern border provinces, which Mr. Thaksin Chinnawat dislikes, coupled with the order to dissolve the SBPAC. This led to an increase in violence, which was considered a mistake in the decision-making of the Thaksin government at that time.

In fact, many local government officials, especially teachers, moved out of the area according to the policy of the Minister of Education at that time, "Mr. Adhisai Phothamarik." Asked if it was because the serious incidents that had been happening continuously for more than 40 years had caused enormous damage to the society, economy and education of the 3 southern provinces. Should we ask ourselves who told the story? How can we benefit from these situations? These are questions that Thai people all over the country want to know.

Of course, according to the knowledge of the villagers or traveling journalists and administrators, the central part that did not know the details criticized and gave opinions according to their knowledge. As for his situation, the writer and the writer's eldest brother were present at the event all the time until the brother died because of his love for our land. The governor of Pattani Province has strongly guaranteed the safety of The writer's brother's life, saying, "Don't worry about anything at all. We will do our duty and be fair to the incident that happened."

The perpetrators tried to shoot the older brother and the assistant, Phi Kiang Chantrat, 3 times already, but the government officials did not do anything to protect the older brother's life. In the end, the perpetrators secretly shot the writer's older brother until he died along with the assistant. Help another person or the governor who once promised It is appropriate to guarantee the safety of the writer's brother's life, in the end, it is just "talking in front and leaving the dog behind," meaning that the governor is a fish with two glasses of water (fake in front and fake in back)

The author tries to dig deep into the cause of the brother being shot, sleeping in the middle of the ground and eating in the sand for a long time, trying to find out the secret that happened to the brother and the southern brothers in the past in a subtle way together with a senior officer, who was the Chief of Staff (Col. Surasak Sonsue) during the time of Pol. Col. San Chitpatima, who has written in the jungle, in and out of military camps and police stations, interviewed villagers, merchants, farmers, and students to find out the details of the clever assassination and to know the secret information and true feelings of our southern people and found that some said that it was the work of those who lost their interests both abroad and in the country. In addition, the spread of news that the military was the one who created the situation occurred. This strategy was rapid and successful because it made the image of the soldiers look scary and could easily create a united front.

Note: Based on the information and insights of the news that was the cause of the brutal murder of the author's brother by bombing him, the author believes in the theory of the united front that was widely reported as the work of the military. In fact, it is an act of the opposite party that is against the power of the state, which is the act of the guerrilla movement to create hatred and seek allies, as mentioned above.

Of course, in our world, whether in Europe, America, the Middle East, Asia, Africa, or the southern part of Thailand, there are many different ideas and opinions on this land. The differences between humans in this world and in our southern land are not the cause of division, or the writer thinks that living together on the same ship in the middle of an ocean of differences is a virtue, a beauty of the water of differences that the world Created for us to live and see the beauty of the differences of human beings since the beginning.

If we go to a flower shop or walk around a flower garden where gardeners grow many types of flowers in the same garden, the various types of flowers will become natural art that decorates the garden, impresses the viewer to be beautiful and impressive. In the same way, the differences between humans are beautiful.

Assistant Professor Dr. Pongthep Suthirawutthi, Director of the Southern Health Research Institute, Prince of Songkla University, presented the problems and solutions to the southern border crisis in an interesting Matichon newspaper as follows:

In political science, society and politics are facing a context of terrorism. Violence is sweeping the world. If we combine economics and social sciences, we will find that the cause is likely to come from the trend of justice, exploitation that undermines the foundations of society, leading to the closure of the channels for creating true justice in society, causing the groups of those who are When the perpetrators retaliate with violence, and when the state's reaction is violent, it is inevitable that a social tragedy will follow.

Although the use of violence in some situations is necessary, it will have negative consequences, such as hatred, resentment, and division, that are difficult to heal. Creating new norms for solving problems using peaceful methods and building reconciliation is, therefore, a balanced approach to the situation. The violence in the 3 southern border provinces and 4 districts of Songkhla Province, historically and socially, is believed to be a desire to separate. The land to be freed from the need for national integration that was acted upon by the central policy, which is the need to maintain the identity of being Malay, being Pattani, which is more than maintaining being Muslim. The urge that is the catalyst for the need for liberation is the injustice of the people in the 3 southern border provinces that have never been received and have been neglected all along.

Now, the situation has become more and more serious. The incident is not only the action of the state and the separatist movement but also the counter-action of many other groups in the area, including many other armed forces, including Thai Buddhist and Thai Muslim groups, who have risen up to protect themselves and have responded. At the same time, The 3 southern border provinces still have influential groups, including politicians, drug groups, and illegal loggers, who are involved in creating situations that make the violence more severe. It is more complex and difficult to solve the problem.

While the state focuses on security, it still copes with the changing situation. The various measures that are not in time to solve the problem? In addition to not being able to solve the situation, it also makes the problem worse. This may be because it is a threat that the security side is not familiar with and does not know what measures to use to solve the problem. Therefore, it still sticks to the old problem-solving methods that it believes will be successful before. At the same time, the corporate culture itself also causes the good suggestions of non-commissioned officers who think outside the box to be neglected.

The old belief that security can solve the problem has been proven that it cannot solve the problem alone. It is necessary to rely on other sectors to help solve the problem. All sectors must urgently create and adjust problem-solving strategies.

At the same time, the voices of the local people who are suppressed by fear will also show their power. When delving deeper into the complexity of the social context in the area, it was found that the important sectors that play a role in solving the overall problem are:

The government sector, security agencies such as the military, police, the Ministry of Interior, and the Southern Border Provinces Administrative Center (SBPAC). In addition to the strategies to build confidence, For the people in the unclear areas, the phenomenon that occurred is clear. It is because the work still lacks coordination and lacks common points in the operation. And there are still images of conflict. For other government agencies, such as the education sector and the public health sector, most of the operations are to solve immediate problems and only within the scope of their duties. The image of integration cooperation is not as clear as expected.

National and local political sectors, including political parties and political groups, provincial administrative organizations, municipalities, and sub-district administrative organizations, are still important questions about how these political groups play both problem-solving and problem-solving roles. Starting with the question of what form local governance should take in line with the Muslim context, such as what should the Surau Council be like? How will governance differ from the current structure?

The civil sector, including community organizations and networks with strong strengths, such as groups related to natural resource management, health networks, women's groups, elderly groups, etc., currently cannot work with the government or work in a direction that supports the government. Because whenever they act as symbols of the government, they have the opportunity to be harmed to the point of death. Such as the case of Khru Pipat Dumdeang.

For community leaders, religious leaders in some areas are the rulers, but in some areas, they are the destroyers of the situation. The natural leaders of some areas are oppressed by threats from the opposing side in the midst of the state's failure to protect their safety, so the people choose to live in safety by taking care of themselves and remain indifferent even though they have to endure seeing the wrong that is happening and must join in doing the wrong thing.

Civil society, including the network of public benefit organizations, work in increasingly difficult areas, both in terms of access to the area and safety in working, because the opposing side is considered an obstacle to the mass appeal, so they choose to reduce their role, do not open up much, work in the area is also smaller and ensure safety.

Academic sectors, including educational institutions and academics both inside and outside the area, have tried to create knowledge sets and propose solutions to problems but found that the existing knowledge cannot explain the phenomena that occur in the area correctly, including being unable to present concrete solutions from the existing knowledge, causing Past solutions to problems to use information that is not up-to-date, mostly relying on beliefs and opinions.

Media Sector Amidst the news flow, both factual and rumor, in the area where the media plays a very important role in providing people in society with correct information, knowledge and understanding. However, in the past, the media often presented only one aspect of violence, which unintentionally created bias in society. The media has a lot of information but lacks analysis. Lack of news synthesis to be presented It seems that the media has no clear direction in presenting news to help solve the crisis in the area.

Guidelines for solving the southern border crisis

1. If the historical and social assumption that violence stems from the ideology of liberation and separatism is true, which is a conflict of ideas, negotiation should be a peaceful solution. But the key question is: Who is the negotiator? Who is negotiating? What are the proposals for negotiation?

Normally, the disadvantaged party is the one who proposes the negotiation. In the current situation, both the government and the opposing party think that they are the advantageous party and can control the situation. The opportunity for negotiation must come from the mediator. At the same time, we must try to create proposals for negotiation from the public from the community, using the media as a medium to communicate with all parties.

2. If historical and social assumptions are true, but the situation has gone too far due to hatred, resentment and division among all parties, negotiation must occur together with compensation for the damage and compensation for the impacts that have occurred both to individuals and must be done simultaneously with society. The compensation must be done sincerely by all parties involved. Especially the local government and community sectors and should act with purity.

3. If the assumption is that violence is caused by the use of ideology as a tool to seek and protect the benefits of those who want power on both sides, the violence of the situation has caused many groups to gain benefits. Solving the problem for peace and happiness will not happen because peace is not the goal of the interest groups. It is very important that the public sector, the social sector, and the academic sector

they must show themselves, join forces to show their stand and join in solving the problem in order not to become a tool. The hand of one party

The author and co-author agree with the above solutions and have the opinion and support for the solution to the southern border problem, which Colonel Patcharawat Thanapran Singh of the Royal Thai Army has presented as a thesis to the War College of the United States Army under the topic: Solving the Conflict Problem in the Southern Border Provinces In the Strategic Project of the US Army War College, with Colonel Allen D. Raymond as advisor and consultant on March 25, 2552.

In conclusion, the conflict in Thailand's southern border provinces is an issue that has a significant impact on Thailand's security both domestically and internationally. There is no specific approach that can be used as a successful formula to solve this problem. However, it must be solved by an integrated approach in a short period of time before the conflict escalates into a war that is difficult to solve.

The resolution of such conflicts must be carried out in an integrated manner, with an emphasis on legal legitimacy and efforts to create unity among the civilians, military and police, in line with the royal ideology of His Majesty King Bhumibol Adulyadej, which is "Understand, Reach and Develop."

If it appears that the attempts to solve the problem by such methods are not successful, the special administrative jurisdiction or the autonomous region should be taken into consideration because the conflict in the border provinces does not grow by itself, is not an international Hajj movement, and that can be solved by Thai people.

However, the researchers of the project suggest that receiving constructive assistance from friendly countries such as America should be acceptable, and all Thai people from all sectors must actively participate in political interests in order to resolve the conflict problem in the southern border provinces of Thailand, where Thai people are waiting to see lasting peace and happiness.

Efforts to resolve the conflict in the province The border has not been continuously implemented. It is well known historically that Pattani was once a kingdom The kingdom was ruled by a monarchy called the Sultans, which succeeded the dynasty of Raya Pattani, totaling 7 kings. As written by a German traveler named Mandel Slohe in the 16th century, "The Kingdom of Pattani at that time was very prosperous and difficult to compare with other Malay cities, even Ayutthaya." Which was the capital of the Kingdom of Siam in the same era was also less prosperous in trade than Pattani. For this reason, the King of Siam aimed to dominate Pattani.

Historically, there were 4 wars between Pattani and Siam. With Siam's military power that was superior to Pattani's, when the war ended, the King of Siam's army rounded up the people and property of Pattani people and brought them to the capital as slaves and followers in large numbers. In 1902, Pattani lost its power. Such a complete cessation of rule meant the loss of sovereignty for all the kings, and The people of Pattani had the rights, freedom and independence under the power of the King of Siam completely.

In 2476, the Thai government declared the dissolution of all the provinces within the country and retained only the status of provinces. As a result of this change, all provinces were directly under the central government, including Yala, Pattani and Narathiwat. With this change, Pattani became a full part of the Kingdom of Siam, which led to greater distance between Pattani and the other Malayan states.

The Constitution provides in its first article that "The Kingdom of Siam is one and indivisible Kingdom."

This provision has a direct impact on Pattani Muslims. The interpretation of this provision of the constitution is strictly nationalistic, meaning that all Thais must use the same language, dress, and religion. This is a huge misinterpretation of the government officials, which has led to hatred and resistance to government power ever since.

In 1934, Luang Phibun Songkram, the Prime Minister at that time, seriously supported this nationalism. He issued a law requiring all Thai people to dress like Westerners, both men and women, to wear hats and forbidding Muslims from dressing according to Malay culture. Buddhism was also the only national religion. The objective is to resolve conflicts and create unity in the Kingdom.

The result caused hatred towards the Siamese government and resistance from that time onwards. This was the first major mistake in solving the problem.

Gen. Prem Tinsulanonda and the conflict in the southern border provinces

The resolution of the conflicts in the southern border provinces during the time when General Prem Tinsulanonda was the Prime Minister by implementing the "Cool Under the Shade" policy into the management was considered the most successful in the history of the present (Modern history)

The Cool Down Policy was a measure adopted by the government to solve the problem of unrest and suppress groups that were opposing the power of the state, namely, the communist terrorist groups, the terrorist bandits, the Malayan communist bandits, and various bandit groups in the southern region during 2524-2527.

The Essence of the Under the Shade Policy

1. To fight to defeat communism as quickly as possible in all respects By political aggression, emphasizing all operations to suppress and destroy the united front movement and armed forces to end the situation, to Create a situation of national war with a neutral policy and expand From the opportunity that is open to change the direction of fighting with arms to fighting In a peaceful way.

2. Political aggression means the destruction or elimination of political conditions or war conditions before the Communist Party of Thailand uses the conditions to create the basic masses to join the movement. Political aggression is the destruction of the party line and the termination of the armed struggle, which ultimately results in the termination of the revolutionary war of the Communist Party of Thailand.

And when General Han Leenanont assumed the position of the 4th Army Commander, he said to the media, "I will go and solve the problem. I will be fair to all parties, whether they are civil servants, soldiers, or police. They must unite. The people who do not receive fairness must find a way to solve the problem."

The influential person sought information on what conditions caused the division between Thai Muslims and Thai Buddhists. We must eliminate it. Relations between Thais and Malaysians must be elevated. Good for each other.

The Cool South Policy is an idea that will bring peace to our brothers and sisters. The peace and coolness of our brothers and sisters in the South will only happen if we have solid cooperation and understanding. Between the government officials who are the ruling party and the people who are the ruled party, and if this can be done, it will be possible to solve the problems of communist terrorism, banditry, Malayan communist bandits and various bandit groups successfully. The problem of terrorism that has been suppressing and destroying the national security in the South will be eliminated.

In order to achieve the goal of the concept and strategy to defeat the enemy of the nation in the southern part of Thailand, Prime Minister's Office Order No. 66/2523 and the 4th Army Region Order No. 751/2524 stipulate that all relevant government agencies, including civil servants, police officers, and military officers, strictly comply with the following:

1. Create safety for the lives and property of the people. All groups, regardless of race and religion, whether Thai Buddhists or Thai Muslims, will be protected from threats from terrorists, communists, terrorist gangs, Chinese Malayan communists and various groups of thieves.

2. Make the Thai-Malaysian border area a safe area to establish and revive the economy of the southern border provinces and raise the level of good relations between Thailand and Malaysia to a higher level.

3. Eliminate authoritarian power, influence and dark power that dominate the atmosphere peacefully and peacefully so that all groups of people have rights, freedom and equality in politics, economics and society under the democratic regime with the King as the Head of State

4. To create good relations between the ruling authorities and the people who are ruled and eliminate the division between the authorities and the people. At the same time, to perform duties to achieve the goal under the cool shade, the 4th Army Area and the Internal Security Operations Command have carried out various actions, such as creating legitimacy, creating social pressure, political training, and mobilizing the people. And the expansion of the scope of power

Gen. Prem Tiinsulanond was born in the South and was once the commander of the 2nd Army Area, which was located in Nakhon Ratchasima Province. He played an important role in the fight to defeat the Communist Party in the Northeast. Therefore, when he was the Prime Minister who was responsible for taking care of and solving the country's problems, including the problems in the southern border provinces, the government at that time analyzed that solving the problems of the Threats cannot be suppressed alone. However, development must be used to lead to suppression. And there is a policy to solve the problem in 2 aspects: development and suppression. By establishing the Southern Border Provinces Administrative Center under the Ministry of Interior and the development and establishment of the 43rd Police Battalion or the 43rd Combined Civilian-Police-Military Command, directly reporting to the 4th Army Area Commander to oversee suppression.

The Southern Border Provinces Administration Centre, known in English as the Southern Border Provinces Administration (SBPAC) or "SBPAC", was established in.

The policies of the government during the reign of General Prem Tiinsulanond, which were implemented by implementing the Cool Southern Policy and the policy of establishing the Southern Border Provinces Administrative Center to solve the conflict problems in the southern border provinces, have been highly effective, resulting in peace and coolness. Terrorism and various forms of violence have gradually decreased to a very satisfactory level.

Mr. Chuan Leekpai and the conflict problems in the southern border provinces

During the time when Mr. Chuan Leekpai was the Prime Minister, the resolution of the conflict in the southern border provinces was carried out in accordance with the footsteps of General Prem Tinsulanonda, emphasizing politics leading the military, which is development along with suppression. The result of implementing the politics-leading-military policy resulted in a significant decrease in conflict and violence in the southern border provinces, with the level of violence reduced to It happens only about 10 times a year.

As stated in the debate of Mr. Chuan Leekpai in the House of Representatives on 27 March 2008, while he was the opposition in the motion of no confidence in the Thaksin Shinawatra government, it can be summarized as follows:

"I am a Southerner by birth. I have been closely acquainted with the culture, attitudes and ideas of southerners as a representative of the people of Trang Province for many eras. I have never failed an exam even once. However, I have seen the mistakes in solving the violence problem in the southern border provinces. The information reported by the officials does not reflect the truth of the events that have occurred in the southern border provinces. The government does not study history. To the cause of the violence that occurred, it will use the same method to solve the problem as it did in the North and the Northeast. It will not be consistent with the reality that occurred in the South and cannot be used to solve the problem in the South."

Pattani was once a prosperous kingdom before becoming a tributary of the Kingdom of Siam. At the same time, in the north, Chiang Mai became a tributary of the Lanna Kingdom. Chiang Mai's becoming a tributary of the Lanna Kingdom did not cause the same resistance and violence as in the Pattani Kingdom because of the traditions, and Chiang Mai's culture is consistent and similar. The people have the same way of life and the same spoken language.

But on the contrary, in Pattani Kingdom, because most of the people are Muslims, the traditions, culture and way of life are very different from Siam Kingdom. In addition, the people in the Pattani Kingdom also wanted to regain independence, so they fought against the state all the time.

Severe to this day and there is still no clear solution. If the government just pays attention to the royal policy of King Rama VI, which he announced to be used in the administration of Pattani, it will be a good solution as follows.

1. Any procedure or practice that causes citizens to know or see as oppressing Islam must be immediately canceled and discarded. Any new arrangement must not conflict with Islamic fundamentalism or, moreover, cause it to be seen as promoting Islam.

2. Any form of scrutiny, taxation, or free-for-all is good when considered as a whole but should not be more than that of the citizens of the nearby British vassal states by such criteria, which is fair; but, when considered in particular, should not be more than that of each other, and therefore is considered a cause of administrative damage.

3. Oppression of government officials and employees due to the unfair use of power is good, but also because of the humiliation and despise of foreign citizens because they are foreigners, and because of the delay in the activities that cause inconvenience to the people in making a living, must be corrected and careful not to let it happen. When it happens, the wrongdoers must be held accountable. The consequences of wrongdoing are not just to cover it up and make it go away but to save face and preserve the dignity of the civil servants.

4. All activities that the officials must command the people must be careful not to cause the people to have to interfere with their own lives to the extent that it is necessary. Even if it is necessary by regulation, there must always be an official present to help and correct it as much as possible.

5. Officials who will be appointed to positions in Pattani Province should only select those who are honest, sincere, calm, and cool. Do not just send them to fill positions or send them as punishment for being bad. When sending them, they must be instructed and explained to them. The characteristics that should be observed carefully by the principles mentioned in points 1, 3 and 4 above. The local adults should continuously train and instill these virtues, not waiting for mistakes to happen and then punish.

6. As planned, it is correct and appropriate for the time and place and shall be considered as a regulation for the administration of Pattani Province from now on.

The author would like to invite you to the royal speech of King Rama VI, who said, *"The problems in the southern part of Siam seem to have existed for a long time and have persisted in every era until present-day Thailand. The problems still exist as if they were mountains. The volcano that will erupt at the right time Perhaps it is time for us to solve this long-standing problem by learning from the past that reflects the present and the present that will affect the future."*

Thaksin Shinawatra and the Prime Minister who is Thaksin's nominee
With the problems of the 3 southern border provinces

As mentioned, Prime Minister Thaksin's administration said that The conflict in the southern border provinces was a huge mistake. The phrase "petty bandits" leads to a huge mistake in giving orders. Believing that the police report was able to control the situation, the police were the reason for the disbandment of the Southern Border Provinces Administrative Center. There were killings, including the Krue Se incident, which created increased hatred.

Gen. Prayut Chan-o-cha as NCPO leader and the Prime Minister and the solution of the problems in the southern border provinces

General Prayut Chan-o-cha seized power on November 22, 2014, by announcing the enforcement of martial law nationwide to resolve the political conflicts that had violently conflicting groups taking over the country.

One of the urgent policies is the policy to quickly put out the southern insurgency, which will bring peace to the southern brothers and sisters quickly and has assigned General Udomdej Sitabutr, who later became the army commander, to be responsible for solving the southern border problems.

General Udomdej Sitabutr has set a policy that he will proceed to solve the problem to be seen as concrete within one year with the motto that says, "Join hearts and start seriously for the nation and the throne," which must receive cooperation from all sectors to lead the various situations to be better.

This has set a guideline for solving the problems in the southern border provinces as a national agenda and has urged the army to control the situation in the area and not neglect matters that are not in accordance with the law and has called on various groups, including those who disagree with the government, to give them a chance and understand each other, and then come and talk to the government by introducing a reform approach by having those who disagree propose their opinions on how to reform the country.

One of the most important policies is the policy on the monarchy, which has always been in the hearts of the military and the people. It does not allow those who do not wish well to cause damage because the monarchy has always been with the Thai people, with Thailand, which has always taken care of the people and the land of Thailand. As a soldier, one must take care of and maintain this monarchy, and it must be consistent with the verse written.

The poems of the patriotic sayings that were written in the media are as follows:

Thais don't love Thaksin. It's not strange.

Thais don't love Abhisit. It's not strange.

Thais don't love the Red Shirts, it's not strange.

Thais don't love the Yellow Shirts, it's not strange.

But if Thais don't love the King, is it strange or not strange? I don't know.

But I say that you shouldn't have been born a "Thai."

9
Closing remarks

Intarakiat Rodpradit, a co-author, was invited to visit to collaborate on this important work that became a book. On a hot day at the end of summer in America, the weather was similar to the summer weather in Thailand, but there was still a warm wind blowing on our bodies, cooling us down there.

We had Brother Chin Jaruek, Big Brother and other guests, including Patty, the writer's wife. We organized a summer BBQ party, which the writer loves. Outdoor activities are a part of the writer's life, and organizing the outdoor BBQ party that day was to welcome the writer and his friend Sarawat Jaruek Sam-angsri.

And will continue to organize activities like this throughout the summer to apply the American European style of living to new friends to experience the atmosphere In the yard in front of our house that day, it was full of freshness and Being together amidst various flowers, roses, daisies and Flowers of all kinds, both direct from Thailand and from Jamaica, from Italy, and found in America, such as from Florida, under the shade of many large trees that stand tall on the edge of the fence of the house that provides warmth from the hot American summer air. Our yard is full of evergreen trees, such as apple trees, Asian cedar trees, Italian plum trees, and bamboo trees around our lawn fence. The cold wind started to blow all the time.

In the sky, there were birds, ducks, and birds flying back and forth in an orderly manner. It looked very beautiful. The sound of those birds was like natural music. It made our barbecue party that day an atmosphere of friendship. The bright lights from the lights we prepared to welcome our two special guests from Thailand. It was not strange to have lights for New Year or Christmas around our house and nearby. The house had a national flag. The American and Thai flags fluttered in the wind on the flagpole, and a large umbrella was beautifully placed to protect the author's favorite pets, BOO-BOO and his cat Sammy, who had previously died. It didn't take long for the two special guests to arrive in America due to a rare eye disease that a veterinarian could save in time.

The author has loved pets since childhood and considers every pet as a member of the family. The author has traveled the world with one of his favorite dogs, and the co-author of this book was the one who arranged for Patta, a smart three-legged dog, to be sent back to the author in Portland by plane. Since the author had to travel back to America suddenly when he went to Thailand for a vacation more than 40 years ago, he understood the author's love and bond with all pets very well, as the American magazine Pet Companion said that the author is one of the greatest pet lovers in America.

And in the conversation, the co-authors affirmed this truth. Even the Lord Buddha, when he was fed up with the conflict between the Dharma and the Vinaya, left seclusion and went to live in the forest with the lions as his friends and followers, and it was clearly evident, even though he was very angry. His Majesty also loves all his pets. Often, when he goes out to a great meeting, Khun Thong Daeng, the dog, will appear. Please stay by his side always.

The author, therefore, always thinks that Thai people should love each other more. For this reason, the author has buried the bodies of both his favorite pets on the lawn in front of his house and has raised the Thai and American flags. Above the graves of both of them to honor and dedicate merit to the souls of both of them to go to a good place. On the graves of both of them, the author has arranged for incense sticks and candles to be lit bright all the time under a large umbrella 24 hours a day throughout the year until the anniversary of their passing, even making inscriptions. He asked curiously, "Dr. Sompong Dumdeang, why did you always light incense sticks and candles on the graves of the two animals? For what reason?"

It is not surprising that Sarawat Jaruek would have such questions because Jaruek does not have enough senses to perceive spiritual life as the writer has experienced. The writer has a sixth sense of the spirit of the animals with whom he has been close and communicated spiritually. It is, therefore, difficult for Jaruek to understand the mysterious spiritual relationship. These writers love animals, whether wild or domesticated, whether they are animals on land or in water, love nature, and consider themselves to be environmental lovers or conservationists, love their friends, and love their neighbors.

At the party for the writer and his friends from Thailand that day, the writer invited his friends, including the English, Russians, and Spanish, to join the party.

That day, it was an international atmosphere with Thais, Vietnamese, and South Americans. Some of them had rented the writer's house before. We had a private party in front of the fire, in front of the writer's house, with Luk Big, a young man from Krabi who is studying intensive English to prepare for university. His goal is to study law in the writer's footsteps. He is a beer provider and server, both Mexican beer and Washington State's Rainier beer, which has a flavor similar to our hometown Singha beer, which is especially prominent at the event.

Luk Big has a high skill in mixing liquor (Kalua) that has a good taste that suits everyone. The writer even praised Luk Big should turning to studying food and beverage service. The future will go very far. We talked and talked to each guest in a friendly manner. When it was time, the neighbors said goodbye and went back. As for us, 3-4 People sit and drink, eat and chat. Continue with some tidbits.

One of the issues that the author asked about was what the word context in English meant in Thai. The author explained to the author that he truly understood that it was the word context.

The author then talks about the issue of conflict crisis in the South, saying that the situation in the South of Thailand in every era and every government has always been a challenge for those responsible for security, whether talking about the Anti-Communist War or the Cold War, the post-Cold War era, and the present, which is The era of terrorism, whether the Cold War or the Terror War, was influenced by the outside world, both directly and indirectly, from Saudi Arabia, Afghanistan, Indonesia and Malaysia.

For example, in the horrific incident that occurred in Paris, France, where 17 people were killed on January 7, 2015, the criminal leaders were trained in Yemen. This is the International context.

The international context occurs both domestically and in the three southern border provinces of Thailand at present. Therefore, the author emphasizes these things. It is a good reflection that the southern problems, such as those that the Thai state in the 21st century must face at present, are not new issues. Rather, they are issues that the Siamese state has tried to find a way through various methods in the past.

As stated in the Manual of Policy Coordination for Pattani Province, 1923, after the history that came to pass, even though the case of "globalization" or the international context in southern Thailand after the Cold War ended, 1989-1990, globalization is a phenomenon of "world trends" that followed. Such trends are mainly economic. We study back to the Cold War era when weapons were the symbol of building security. Every state in the world focused on "arms accumulation," but in the globalized world, every state focused on "arms accumulation." Compete to accumulate stability," but the government has neglected to cut the budget to stability. The enemy will have a chance to intervene and attack to destroy the stability and stability of the country more easily.

For example, the heated incident in Paris, France, on January 7, 2015, was a huge disaster that reverberated throughout the world. The world attacked France, saying that the French government had ordered a budget cut for the security accumulation because France thought it was not necessary because its security was already secure enough. When the security budget was cut, there were not enough personnel at this level to protect the country. The problem was solved without any timeliness. Now, France has declared war on the terrorists, just like our country. Cows disappearing in cow pens It is the opposite of the horrific incident that happened in Paris, France, which is a good lesson for the world, including the southern part of Thailand.

Therefore, such a phenomenon occurred in France because France did not sit back and prepare for the new era of the world. The new era is stability, which will be the path to the stability of the French state. The writer knows this well and suggests that, in fact, such a phenomenon is a reflection of The phenomenon of paradigm change. As the Buddha always warned us, everything in this world is impermanent, of course, but changes, including society, politics and the environment around us.

Professor Preedee Panomyong wrote about the history of politics, society, and human beings. We often fall into a state of change from monarchy to dictatorship, etc. It cannot bring permanent stability to the world situation. We can make something impermanent permanent. We must let it be according to "dharma," or as we know it, let it be as it is.

The author briefly emphasizes that the post-Cold War world is a world that is under initial economic globalization. But the family must have a car, a good house, a good marriage, a good job, good health, good public health, good education, a TV, a mobile phone, etc. From the family is a society, society is a country, turning to compete with each other in the way of "globalization," the economy is the main guarantee of life. Family Insurance Country Insurance To avoid being inferior to neighboring countries or civilized countries as follows:

Therefore, readers may follow and agree with the author who said that it seems that globalization in terms of security is an issue that has been overlooked by implication. Why? Because of the belief or "post-Cold War globalization" that sees the end of the confrontation between the new nuclear superpowers, namely the United States and the Soviet Union, making the present world, the new world, step into the era of true peace, at least the chance of a major war like the World War or even a nuclear war between the two superpowers has ended.

Now, let's assume that there is no more war. If there was a war after the Cold War, what would be the cause? When it comes to conflict, conflict is common everywhere in every corner of the world that we humans live in, which is fashionably called the world's international conflict, World War II or Major War.

Now, between the Western world and the Muslim world, including our Muslims in the South, Because the South is a part of the world, the world is a part of the South (International contact to Southern Thailand), World events are caused to clash abroad, which are related to political relations, and reflect as a transparent light to the 3 southern provinces of Thailand that cannot be avoided because changes in the world have an influence on the South Events such as those that occurred in France on January 17, 2015, and those that have occurred in general in Europe, America, Africa, Nigeria, Yemen, and in America, such as the terrorist attacks on a commercial building in New York, are a global horror. It also affected 3 southern border provinces of Thailand.

Therefore, when there is a context of the world situation and the new organization's stability, it is very important. Therefore, the state must carefully consider how to resist "against the resisters, against terrorism." The state must use its wits and intelligence. It cannot use emotions in a modern way. Why? Because it leads the Thai state into a war trap. The process of extreme suppression is like the state digging itself the grave and burying itself, or the state digging itself the Grave, making it impossible to withdraw as it is now.

However, readers should not misunderstand the author as not wanting the government to do anything or not to take any action. This does not mean that the southern fire will continue to simmer. However, the methods to solve the Southern fire problem, no matter what form or direction, as long as it is implemented, will not lead to success.

Therefore, both writers try their best to propose social suppression using military suppression, people's military war, people's war, people's war, and other methods that may lead to nuclear war between the two superpowers, which has ended and the government is doing everything at present to solve the southern insurgency problem.

Both authors have collected extensive data bases, applied to the main issues of His Majesty King Rama IX, understood and developed. For the problems that have occurred, development that will be solved according to the conditions of "reality" will depend entirely on "rumored" news or intelligence. Implementation without knowing which direction to go in is not the policy and practice of the state at all, and the state should not adhere to such a. Amata is stuck with old policies that have failed in the past. The conditions, policies and implementation ideas of the government should be in accordance with our proposals as follows:

History

- Back to 1923, the history of the Pattani Kingdom
- Consider the problems, processes, and the underlying perspectives and ideas.
- It is a proposal to the government to see the wrong practices by using the resolution of strategy.
- Military, with an emphasis on small wars, or what locals and the general public know as "counter-insurgency."
- The chaos, the disadvantages of the state's abrogation of rights in a crisis situation, such as, for example, when Prem established "Reconciliation Under the Cool Shade," why? Because it caused the Thai state to enter a war trap with the process of extreme suppression. It would be like the state digging a hole to bury itself or the state making it unable to withdraw, as it is now.

"The political factor that indicates the lack of success or failure of the implementation is the resistance or collapse of the state mechanism and the international power." It has almost brought peace to our 3 southern provinces, but Thaksin has destroyed and canceled it. Such behavior is not for the benefit of the southern people, not for the benefit of the country, but for the personal benefit of Thaksin because of his selfishness. The power that Thaksin has is 100% because it was divided to lose Thaksin's power. Therefore, it destroys the good program of the southern people because, during this time, the strong leaders and the coconut heads who are the terrorists have reported themselves to the government and are ready to join the government. The unity and harmony are starting to occur like the bright light of the Sun. It is shining on our southern people.

- Experimenting with new concepts, which are called perspectives, such as Applying new strategies for the southern border provinces. Both authors give their thoughts on establishing a security organization with a new perspective for this area.
- Hope for stability and security in the future of the southern border provinces.
- Get water and point out the solution to the problem in the international context.

"Southern International Resolution"

Both writers would like to implore this government to be especially capable of solving the Southern problems in a thorough and thorough manner in all cases and events. It should not be done only halfway or only to reduce or alleviate the problems, which will have little or no results at all. It must truly bring peace to the country and find a dimension to create unity between our Thai and Muslim brothers and sisters and create peace and harmony, including Perfect happiness among all communities, all religions, all genders, and all ages.

Look at the history of our neighbors, such as India. The problem of the summer solstice in India was solved by a great leader, Mahatma Gandhi. The principle of nonviolence. The problem of skin conflict was solved by Lincoln. The problem of abolishing slavery was solved by King Rama V. In Thailand (His Majesty King Bhumibol Adulyadej), Lincoln also abolished slavery in the United States.

Therefore, the crisis problem in the South should not be solved. Only humans can create the problem. Humans themselves must solve the problem. We do not need to refer to Allah. It is pointless. We as a whole nation must help solve the problem under the royal address of the Queen to the masses. This book is almost like a manual between the government and the people. Both writers would like to reiterate that the Southern fire problem is something we must address (all problems can possibly be solved). Solving the problems of the Southern fire, national problems, and world problems is the responsibility of all of us. As long as we share the air we breathe, all of us will have a part and a duty to solve the problems of the country, the city, and the world together. It is not just the responsibility of the government, but it is not just us sitting around, dreaming, and imagining to help each other solve the problems with us, and we must. We should not only receive help from the government. But it is the opposite that we have to ask ourselves the question: What good have we done for the government? As Kennedy told us in his speech.

"What can you do for your country? Not what country can do for you?"

We must use this idea to solve the South because Kennedy's idea is not only true for Americans but also for society, politics, and humanity around the world, including our southern Thailand.

"Together we can change the world, change the world to be a better place to live because together, we can make the world be difference."

10
Summary and Suggestions for Solving the Problem:
The unrest in the three southern border provinces

Warring parties
Thai state and dissidents

The unrest situation in the three southern border provinces or the southern insurgency refers to the conflicts that have occurred for a long time and are currently ongoing, mostly occurring in the three southern border provinces, especially Pattani, Yala, Narathiwat and the Thai state, and various groups causing unrest. Originally, it was the Pattani Sultanate, which had self-governance before it was re-established. Cultural conflicts thus began and emerged in 2491. It was the beginning of ethnic and religious separatism in the Malay region. Patani has had a low level of separatist violence in the region. As such, for decades, the incident escalated after 2544, with the outbreak occurring from 2547 to 2454, resulting in 4,500 deaths and 9,000 injuries. The nature of the incidents was increasingly aimed at revenge.

The initial insurgent groups aimed to seize and become independent, such as the BNPPI and Pulo groups, where local leaders continuously demanded some degree of independence for the Pattani region and some insurgent movements, such as the BRN and the NPU, some of which called for peace negotiations with the Thai state.

In the past, governments of all eras have given special importance to the three southern border provinces. Although some governments, such as the governments of Pol. Lt. Col. Thaksin Chinnawat and Abhisit Vejjajiva have given less importance to solving the problems. They have accepted that the three southern border provinces have geographical characteristics that are far from the central administrative center. There are areas adjacent to neighboring countries that have similar cultures in terms of society, religion, and culture that are unique to the area where there is unrest, and the problems that are complex and detailed in terms of society, psychology, economics, politics, and governance, have led to misunderstandings and suspicions in the relationship between government officials and the people. Negative attitudes towards each other and misunderstandings between the people and the government officials in the area cause repeated problems and are factors that will cause the government's policies to be successful or fail. In addition, there are also various injustices.

From the problems that have occurred with the people in the three southern border provinces due to the incidents of violence in the past and present, whether they are political problems, the desire to divide the territory, economic problems, psychological problems, educational problems, social problems, justice problems, unemployment problems of the people, and poverty problems, which the people want the government to urgently resolve these problems. These conflicts are the result of History.

First of all, it is a matter that people do not talk about much. It is only a superficial matter that is passed on. But in fact, it is the root of the problem. It is a historical wound, including the injustice in the area that the state itself tries to cover up and swallows up history. In terms of ethnicity, they are the Central Malays. Siam, at that time, had attacked the southern capitals, including Pattani. In the past, and annexed as part of Siam and became a wound for the people in the area because the Pattani ruler did not agree to cause frequent wars, and these histories were told and passed down from generation to generation, just like many Thai people tell their children and grandchildren that the Burmese burned down houses and cities and this is the story of Pattani these are the stories that the state cannot solve. With only military strategy, it is necessary to include a multi-dimensional strategy as a component to solve the problem effectively as follows:

1. Adhere to the strategies of King Rama IX to solve the problems, namely "Understand, Reach, and Develop," including using the Sufficiency Economy Philosophy as a strategy, making it a vision by looking to the future in order to create development and creating sustainable stability based on the foundation of unity amidst social and cultural differences.

2. Military strategy, the determination of the state's policy to solve problems, focusing on military over politics, has proven to be unsuccessful. In fact, a stable state must maintain a strong military to protect the country. However, using military force to suppress people who have different opinions always leads to the opposite result. For example, the incident that reminds us of the pain is the Tak Bai incident that occurred in the year 2003, which ignited the southern fire once again, including the Krue Sae incident, where the state used force to brutally suppress protesters, many people were tortured and forcibly disappeared, causing wounds once again, making the local people feel that they did not receive justice, causing the survivors of the incident to no longer believe in peace. Some groups, therefore, rose up to seize weapons and live in peace. Together with the armed movement in the forest, Ready to fight the state with violence. Therefore, the state must use military strategy together with political strategy, that is, use politics to lead the military in resolving conflicts in the three southern border provinces in line with the proposal of General Ekkachai Srivilai, Director of the Office of Peace and Good Governance, King Prajadhipok's Institute, who said.

"It is certain that the use of military force with weapons to solve the problem will not be able to solve the problem and reduce the violence. On the contrary, if we use the principle of politics leading the military by helping the people to have safety in life and property, not using weapons to solve the problem, but instead

emphasizing development work and creating safety for the lives and livelihoods of the people, it will result in a situation of violence. The intensity can be reduced."

3. Governance strategies to resolve conflicts in the three southern border provinces

The administration of administration in the three southern border provinces must take into account various components that are conducive to solving, improving and developing in order to create peace and happiness for the people in the conflict areas as follows:

3.1 Strengthen trust and cooperation between the government and the people. The importance of selecting and developing officials from all parties to have awareness, attitudes, personalities, and peaceful behaviors, and to respect human rights. To perform duties in the southern border provinces, there is a joint mechanism between the government and the people to monitor and inspect the performance of duties to be strictly within the framework of the law. Develop knowledge, understanding, and skills in coping with conflict and cultural skills for government officials on a regular basis.

3.2 Enhance public confidence in the justice process to occur in a concrete manner and, enforce the law with fairness, and punish the wrongdoers without exception.

3.3 Eliminate conditions and causes that cause people in the area to feel divided or unequal in a concrete way to make people feel happy and have dignity.

3.4 Build trust in the government's remedial process to cover all groups at all levels by developing systems and improving the remedial process to be transparent, fair, non-discriminatory, and without delay, and with a system for inspection, monitoring and evaluation to increase the efficiency of remedial measures, preventing the seeking and benefiting of remedial measures from all parties, including promoting women's groups and the civil society. Society plays a role in the process of redressing the lost and affected.

3.5 Support the central government agencies, regional government organizations, local government organizations, civil society, the public sector, and all stakeholders to participate more in development and solutions by establishing a government management mechanism that has the potential and provide opportunities for all parties to participate in every step of problem-solving and development of the area and participate in the justice process, develop strategies and Operation, plans and projects under the management policy Southern border provinces.

3.6 Support the opening of safe spaces at all levels in a tangible manner. Give the public and stakeholders, both inside and outside the area, the opportunity to express their opinions freely on the basis of mutual trust by having all sectors participate at a level that results in policy changes and truly implements them.

3.7 Promote, support and increase the participation role of women, children and youth at all levels in decision-making to be strong in solving problems and developing areas in all dimensions continuously by developing the use of potential in peace and creativity, driving operations, promoting peace and happiness in families, communities and society on the basis of rights and freedom between women and men.

3.8 Promote the values and acceptance of living together in a multicultural society with dignity, dignity and equality by respecting the values of all religions and ethnicities, fostering relationships with local languages, cultures and education, and instilling morality and ethics in the youth according to the good principles of religion.

3.9 Promote the exchange process of learning for government officials in all sectors to be aware, have a deep understanding, accept and see the value of the cultural identity and life of the local people, including adhering to the principles of understanding religion, language and culture, as well as volunteering, ready to work in the area and organize training to create understanding continuously.

3.10 Promote understanding between people and people in both the area and Thai society to live together peacefully and join forces to solve common problems by opening up communication spaces to create mutual understanding about the real situation in the area and exchange knowledge on living together peacefully despite diversity, especially between children and youth of different religions.

3.11 Promote the way of life and practice of all religions without obstacles by adjusting incorrect attitudes, adjusting laws and regulations to promote stability, living according to religious principles, and eliminating cultural discrimination, and all parties must study, understand and accept the way of life and culture to make people feel part of Thai society.

3.12 Developing the potential of people in society by accelerating the management and development of the quality of education at all levels to truly align with the needs, lifestyles, and cultures of the area. Provide opportunities for religious leaders, qualified persons, and all sectors in the area to participate in making suggestions and managing education to promote the development of knowledge and vocational skills and expand educational opportunities, especially educational scholarships both domestically and internationally that are consistent with In line with the lifestyle and needs of the people and ensure the stable status of personnel who graduated from abroad, as well as develop the potential of the workforce to be in line with the economic status in the area to create opportunities, linking with the development of neighboring countries in the ASEAN Community.

3.13 Accelerate the development of the quality of life of the underprivileged people in the southern border provinces in all dimensions by reaching the people equally and fairly, emphasizing the process of people's participation in line with the problems, needs and characteristics of the society of each area, as well as promoting good relationships and understanding.

3.14 Create opportunities for economic development by developing infrastructure, developing human resources to support economic development in the area, strengthening the main agricultural base from the community, such as rubber, fisheries, etc., to achieve commercial self-sufficiency, supporting the Halal industry, tourism, solving unemployment problems, and providing special privileges to create investment incentives. And promote the role of private businesses to be ready to support the expansion of ASEAN.

3.15 Develop and promote natural resource management in the area to maximize the benefits of quality-of-life development and poverty alleviation by supporting and increasing the roles of the public, civil society, communities and local organizations in the protection, care, allocation and rehabilitation of coastal fisheries, mangrove forests and lowlands, including preventing groups of interests who unfairly exploit resources.

3.16 Promote the learning of Thai, Malay, Malay Local, Arabic and important foreign languages by implementing at all levels of education to be a tool for seeking knowledge, communication and opportunities for development in all aspects, including being an important potential for preparing for communication and relations in the ASEAN Community and the Arab world.

3.17 Decentralize the administrative power appropriately on the basis of pluralism under the intention of the Constitution of the Kingdom of Thailand in accordance with international principles, not a condition leading to a territorial division in the area, and create an environment of confidence and a guarantee of safety in the freedom of expression and discussion of all sectors, reflecting the concerns of people of all nationalities, races and religions.

3.18 Promote the continuity of the dialogue process for peace. The southern border provinces with individuals who have different opinions and ideologies from the state to have unity create a guarantee of safety in participating in expressing the opinions of all stakeholders in the dialogue process for peace. The southern border provinces by implementing the plan to drive the dialogue process, Effectively promote peace and happiness in the southern border provinces.

3.19 Enhance understanding with neighboring countries, international organizations and private development organizations about the real facts about the situation in the southern border provinces by expanding the implementation results according to government policies, real facts on the rights, freedom, liberty, equality and equality of people of all races and ethnicities to integrate the relationship in supporting and facilitating the resolution of the problems in the southern border provinces.

4. Strategy, peace and negotiation to extinguish the Southern fire

"I don't agree with violence in any form," *said one peace activist.* "But we believe in the peace process through sincere dialogue between the dissidents and the government."

Both authors would like to commend the government of Ms. Yingluck Shinawatra for initiating negotiations with the insurgents in the three southern border provinces, a decision that was risky and challenging to both failure and success because it was a bold move that risked protests that the government's willingness to be a negotiator would give the disputing parties an opportunity to elevate their status to be accepted on the world stage. But the first negotiation to end violence, with Lt. Gen. Paradorn Pattanathabutr, former director of the National Security Council, as the head of the negotiating team and from the beginning of the first negotiation, created hope for a clear resolution of the southern border problems. The result of the negotiation, when Gen. Prayut Chan-o-cha came to administer the country, continued the idea of peace negotiations with the perpetrators. The unrest with the BRN group as the core, the government of General Prayut Chan-o-cha has supported the opening of negotiations with the BRN group on many occasions, in which both sides have agreed on a common approach to peace based on the 3 principles that will be the substance of future talks, namely:

4.1 Reduce violence

4.2 Consultation with local people

4.3 Seeking political solutions

We, both writers, support the resolution of conflicts in the three southern border provinces through peaceful negotiations and believe that the government is on the right track and sincerely hope that future peace negotiations will lead to a consensus that will lead to lasting peace.

May peace and happiness be established for the people in the three southern border provinces, for the lasting and stable peace and tranquility of the people in the area and for the country as a whole.

Conclusions and recommendations for resolving the conflict in the three southern border provinces of Thailand

THE PARTIES AT WAR
Thai State vs. the Insurgent Movement Groups

The unrest situation in the three southern border provinces of Thailand means the long-standing and ongoing conflicts that mainly occur in the three southernmost provinces, especially in the provinces of Pattani, Yala and Narathiwat and or the Thai State with various insurgent groups which were originally self-govearned sultanate state of Pattani, until the assimilation of the conflicted culture began and manifested itself in 1948 as an insurgence, racial and religious segregation in the Malay Pattani Region. There has been low-level separatist violence in the region for several decades, but it escalated after 2001 with an escalation from 2004 to 2016 with 4,500 deaths, more than 9 persons were injured with the plot aimed at more revenge.

Early insurgent groups aimed at independence, such as the BNPP, Pulo and the PULO, where local leaders continued calls for a degree of autonomy to the Pattani Region and the insurgent movements, including the BRN and some of them called for peace talks with Thai State.

In the past, governments of all ages have given special importance to the areas of the three southern border provinces, such as the government of Thaksin Shinawatra and the government of Abhisit Vejjajiva, although both governments have given less importance to solving the problems of these areas but all have recognized this region as geographically far distance from the central government center of administration and also being adjacent to neighboring countries with similar culture. There is a similar culture in terms of social religion that is a unique characteristic of the unrest area, the condition in which the sensitivity and complexity, in terms of society, psychology, economy, politics and governance, cause misunderstanding and paranoia in the relationship between people and government officials in the area, causing further problems leading to success or failure in implementation. There is also the factor of injustice in several fields that aggravate situations.

From the problems of violent events that occurred to people of three border southern provinces in the past and continuing until at present, whether from the political problem, the insurgent movement groups wanted to divide our land, including the problems in economics, physiological problems, educational problem, social problem, justice problem, unemployment and the problem of property of people of the conflicted areas that need to be urgently addressed by the government as all of these problems of conflicts are the results from history.

The first is something that people don't talk much about. Only superficial was conveyed, but it was actually the root of the problems, the historical wound, as much as the injustice in these areas. The government itself tried to hide and swallow history despite the fact that they are ethnic Malay. The Siamese central government at that time attacked southern cities, including the former state of Pattani, and annexed it to be part of Siam became the wound of people in the area and because the ruler, the sultanate of Pattani refused to surrender, caused frequent battles between the Kingdom of Siam and the state of Pattani and those stories were told and passed on from generation to generation like many Thai people told their children the history that Burma burnt houses and cities and this is storytelling of Pattani. Thai State, therefore, cannot solve these problems of conflict with Military strategy alone, but it is necessary to incorporate multi-dimensional strategies as the component factors to the solution to achieve peaceful purposes and the following strategies are recommended for solution:

History, despite the fact that they are the ethnic Malay. The Siamese central government at that time attacked southern cities, including the former state of Pattani, and annexed it to be part of Siam became the wound of people in the area and because the ruler, the sultanate of Pattani refused to surrender, caused frequent battles between the Kingdom of Siam and the state of Pattani and those stories were told and passed on from generation to generation like many Thai people told their children the history that Burma burnt houses and cities and this is storytelling of Pattani. Thai State, therefore, cannot solve these problems of conflict with Military strategy alone, but it is necessary to incorporate multi-didimensional strategies as the component factors to the solution to achieve peaceful purposes and the following strategies are recommended for solution:

2. Military Strategy. Determining the state's problems-solving with a focus on the military over politics has proven unsuccessful. It is true that a stable state must maintain its military with a strong defense of the country, but the deployment of military forces to suppress dissent has always had the opposite effect. For example, an incident that reminded me of the true pain was the TAK BAI incident in the year 2003, which reignited the southern fire, including the use of force by the government to brutally suppress demonstrators, many of whom have been tortured and forced to disappear, causing wounds again, causing local people to feel that there is no justice for them and causing those who survived the incident to no longer believe in peaceful means anymore. Some groups, therefore, rose up to take up arms and join the armed movement in the forest and fight the state with violence. Therefore, the state has to combine military strategy with political strategy, that is to say, use politics to lead the military to resolve the conflicts in southern areas in compliance with the proposal of Gen. Ekachai Sriwilas, director of the Office of Peace and Governance of King Prapokklao's Institute said

"It is clear that the use of military forces with weapons to solve the conflicted problems will not be the answer to the question and reduce violence. On the other hand, if we apply political strategy to lead the military by means of helping people to have peace of mind and safety in life and property instead of using military forces with weapons to solve the problems of conflict, but focusing on the development, ensuring the safety of people's livelihood will have good results and the violent situation will be gradually reduced."

3. Administrative Strategy: Administrative management in the three southern border provinces needs to take into account the various elements contributing to improvement and development in order to bring peace to the people in conflict areas as follows:

- Strengthen trust and cooperation between the state and the people. The importance of selecting and developing officers from all parties to have awareness, attitude, personality, and peaceful behavior, respect for human rights to perform duties in 3 southern border provinces must be taken into consideration. There must be a joint mechanism between the state and people to stickily monitor the performance of the duties of state officers within the framework of the law, build understanding, developing the skill of encountering the conflict and culture of the state officers continually.

- Build confidence in the process of justice for the people to create fair justice and, enforce the law with equality, bring the offenders to justice without any exception.

- Eliminate conditions and the causes that made people in the area feel divided or inequality in a concrete way so that people will feel happy and dignified.

- Build confidence in the government's remedial process, providing coverage for all groups at all levels by developing and improving the healing process to be transparent and fair, with no discrimination, no delay, maintaining the investigation system, follow up and appraise the results in order to add proficiency of remedy, prevent from seeking the benefit and facilitate the benefit from remedy from all parts, support women's group and social community to participate in the remedial process for the victims and those affected.

- Support for central government agencies, provincial administration, local administration organizations, civil society, public sector and all stakeholder groups to participate in further development and amendment by establishing a potential government mechanism and allowing all parties to participate at all levels in the process of solving problems and developing the areas, take participation in the justice process, developing the strategies, and implement the plans and projects under the southern border provincials administrative policy.

- Supporting the opening of the safe areas at all levels in a concrete way, allowing people and those who are stakeholders both inside and outside the areas to have the opportunity to express their opinion freely on the basis of mutual trust and allowing all sectors take participate at the level effecting the cause of real change as policy and practice.

- Promote, support, and increase the role of women, children, and the youth to participate in decision-making at all levels to strengthen problem-solving and continually develop the areas in all dimensions, developing the use of potentiality in terms of peace and creative operation, support peace in the family, community, and society base on the principle of freedom between women and men.

- Promote the values and the acceptance of multicultural society with dignity and equality, respecting the value of all religions and ethnic, giving importance to language, culture and local education, instill morals and ethnic in youth to the good principles of the religion.

- Promote the process of exchanging understanding to all sectors of government officials to raise their awareness with deep understanding, accept and appreciate the cultural identity and the life of people in the conflicted areas, as well as to extend understanding of religious issues, languages and culture including volunteering spirit ready to work in the areas and also organize training continually to create good understanding.

- Promote understanding between people in the areas and society to coexist peacefully and join forces to help solve problems together by opening communication to create mutual understanding about the real situation in the areas and exchange knowledge of peaceful coexistence based on diversity, especially between the youth of different religions.

- Promote unobstructed ways of life and practice of all religions by adjusting wrong attitudes, adjusting relevant issues to be conducive to stable religious living in accordance with the principle of religion, eliminating cultural discrimination, eliminates cultural discrimination and all parties must study, create understanding and accept in the ways of life and cultural to make people feel they are part of Thai society.

- Develop the potential of people in society by accelerating the management and development of the quality of education at all levels in accordance with the real needs, way of life, and culture of the areas, allowing religious leaders, the experts, and all sectors the opportunity to participate in giving recommendations and educational management, giving support the development of skills knowledge, especially the skills in the professions, expanding educational opportunity, especially the scholarship both at home and aboard to be in line with people's needs and lifestyle, certifying the stable status of those who graduated from abroad, including development labor skills to be in accordance with economics potentiality in the areas in order to link up with the development of neighboring countries in Asian Community.

- Accelerate the development of the quality of life of the underprivileged people in all dimensions of the border provinces by reaching people thoroughly and fairly, emphasizing the process of people's participation in accordance with the problems, needs and social characteristics of the area as well as fostering a good relationship and understanding.

- Create opportunity for economic development by developing infrastructure, developing human resources to support economic development in the area, strengthening the main agricultural development from the community such as rubber, fishing, etc., to be commercially sufficient, supporting HALAL industry, travel industry, solving the problems of unemployment, including the granting of privileges and create incentive for investment and promote the role of private business sector to support the expansion of Asian.

- Develop and promote the management of natural resources in the area for the maximum benefit of improving the quality of life and poverty alleviation by supporting and increasing the role of

- people, civil society community, and local organizations in the protection, allocation, rehabilitation of coastal fisheries, mangrove forests, and flood plans as well as preventing the unfair use of resources by interested groups.

- Promote learning Thai, Malay, local Malay, Arabic, and major foreign languages at all levels of education to be used as a tool in seeking knowledge, communication, and the opportunity for development in all fields, including significant potential in preparing for the readiness in connection with Asian community as well as the Arab world.

- Decentralization of appropriate administrative powers on the basis of plural society under the spirit of the constitution of the Kingdom of Thailand in accordance with international principles, not a condition leading to separation in the area and creating a confidential environment to guarantee the safety in freedom, expression of opinion and dialogue with all parts of all stakeholders reflected to people's worrisome of all races and religions.

- Promote the continuity of the process of dialogue for peace in southern border provinces with people who have different opinions and ideologies from the state, create guaranteed security to participate in the expression of opinions of all stakeholder groups, create operation process for peaceful dialogue by implementation the plan to drive for dialogue process efficiently for improvement the happiness for southern border provinces.

- Enhance good understanding with neighboring countries, international organizations, and NGOs, raising the facts concerning the real situation in southern border provinces by expanding the implementation of government's policies, the fact on the rights and freedom of action, equality, and equality of people of all races for integrate relationship to support in solving problems in the southern border provinces

4. Peace Strategy: Negotiation for the extinction of the Southern fire.

One pacifist said, "I am against all forms of violence, but believe in a peaceful process through sincere dialogue with both dissidents and the state."

Both authors praise the government of MS.Yingluk Shinawatra who initiated counter negotiation with the insurgents in three southern border provinces. It was a risky and challenging decision for the failure and success because it was daring to risk protest that the state's agreeing to be a negotiating partner may cause the dissidents to take advantage of all opportunities to upgrade their status to be accepted on the world stage. The first negotiation to end violence was headed by Lt.Gen. Paradorn Phattanthabutr, former director of the National Security Council, and from that negotiation, there was a hope of solving the problems of conflict. When Gen. Prayuth Chan-O Cha took over the administration of the country, he supported continuing peace negotiations with the insurgent group, and the BRN group was core to participate in a peace dialogue. With his encouragement, peace talks have been taken several times, and both parties have reached a consensus on 3 principles to lead to the next phase of dialogue as follows:

Reduce all kinds of violence. Consultation with people in the area. Seek a political solution.

We, both writers, support the resolution of the problems of conflict in three southern border provinces through peaceful dialogue and believe that the state came on track, and it is hoped that the next peace talks will bring about a consensus that lead to lasting peace in the area.

May the peaceful and tranquility prevail for the people of southern border provinces and for the Thai Nation as a whole.

***

In my personal opinion and based on political experience, the situation in Southern Thailand was more peaceful before the Thaksin regime. Thaksin's leadership mistreated the situation and insulted anti-government groups by publicly labeling and mocking them. Such actions—including derogatory terms like "ทัศอิดลู้หมา"—caused significant unrest, dehumanized the opposition, and led to widespread violence and death.

These uncritical and aggressive actions worsened the conflict, especially from 2004 onward, during the rise of the so-called "hunting luck" regime. The government ignored the increasingly severe and crude conditions in Southern Thailand. It has proven incapable of resolving both longstanding and emerging issues in the region.

I state, clearly and conclusively, that the Yingluck Shinawatra government is now facing significant political and judicial pressures, which may ultimately lead to its removal from office in the coming weeks and months.

In the weeks and months ahead, a more conservative administration might assume power—one more closely aligned with the Democrat Party and the military.

Any such administration would likely face ongoing protests and challenges to its legitimacy, which would limit its capacity to effectively address the southern conflict. In my view, in the medium term, a new government—particularly if it includes figures from the current regime—would likely regard the Thaksin-initiated peace process with skepticism. They might even be tempted to abandon it on partisan political grounds.

That would be a tremendous loss. If the progress made over the past several years were to be discarded by a new Thai administration—such as one that disbanded the Kuala Lumpur peace initiative—it would be devastating.

Given the number of lives already lost in this tragic insurgency, any peace process is better than no peace at all.

If the gains made over the past years were to be squandered by an incoming Thai administration that disbands the Kuala Lumpur initiative, it would be a tragic setback.

Given the number of lives lost in this terrible insurgency, any peace process is better than no peace process at all.

I strongly advise the current regime of my country, Thailand, to uphold and continue pursuing peace efforts for the sake of our people and future generations.

***

Moreover, solving the crisis in Southern Thailand requires a deeper understanding.

Many sources should be considered—especially in terms of language, cultural context, and historical complexity.

The U.S.-based Human Rights Watch issued a report on Tuesday highlighting **22 cases of "disappearances"** that have yet to be investigated. The organization accused the government of failing to hold authorities accountable for past abuses.

Some analysts argue that until the **local Muslim population** feels justice has been served—and is guaranteed—the insurgency will only continue to grow.

The Deep South was once an independent Islamic sultanate called **Pattani**, before the region was conquered by Bangkok in 1786. It was placed under direct rule of the Thai bureaucracy in 1902.

The South's separatist struggle has been fueled by the local population's sense of insurgency.

The Deep South was once an independent Islamic sultanate called **Pattani**, before the region was conquered by Bangkok in **1786**. It was placed under the direct rule of the Thai bureaucracy in **1902**.

The South's separatist struggle has been fueled by the local population's sense of **religious and cultural alienation** from the Thai state.

More than **80 percent** of the two million people in the **three-province region** identify as **Muslims of ethnic Malay descent**. They share closer cultural and religious ties with neighboring **Malaysia** than with the predominantly **Buddhist Thai Kingdom**.

MAP OF THAILAND

Map of Thailand

Map of Southern Thailand

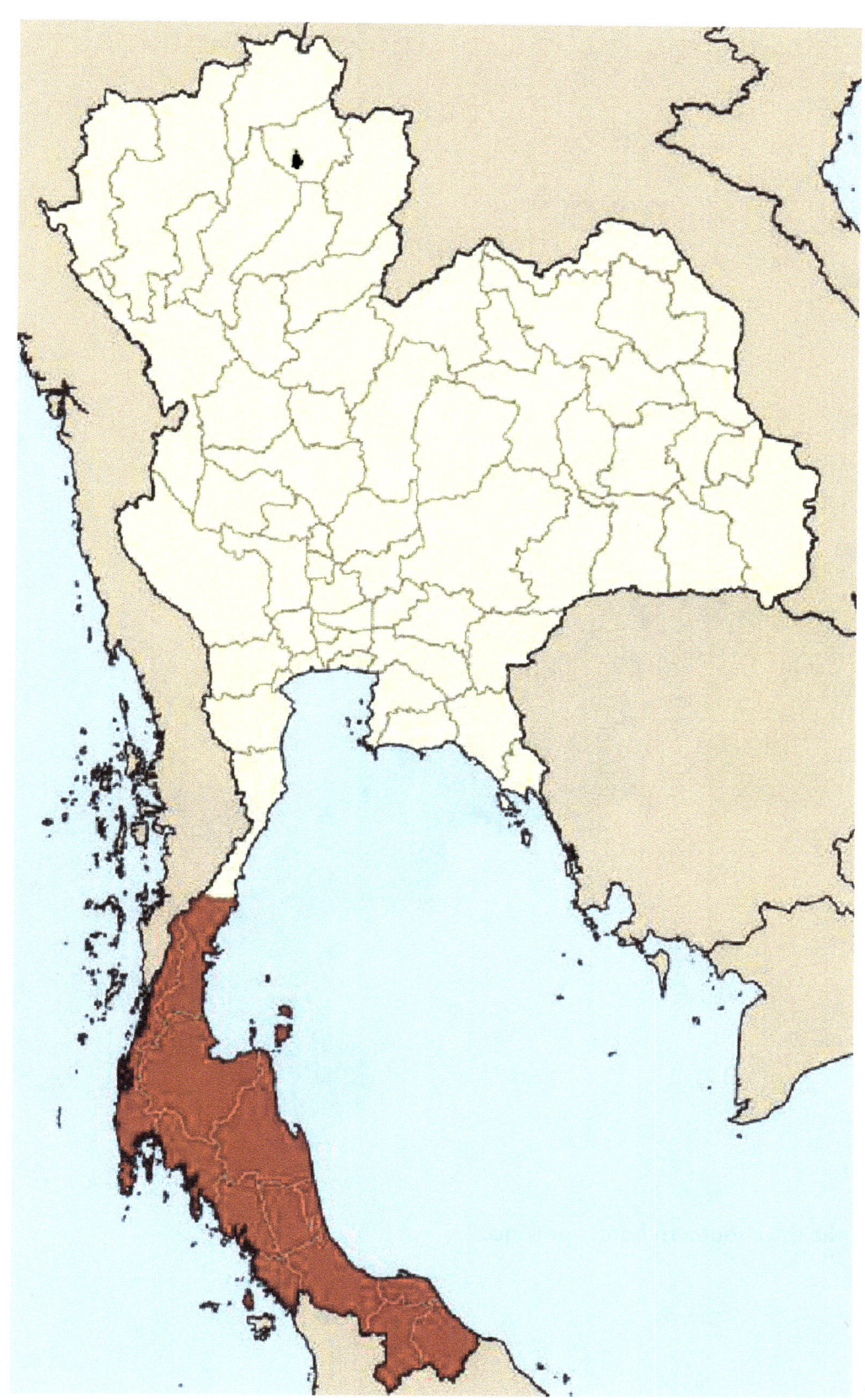

Map of Southern Thailand

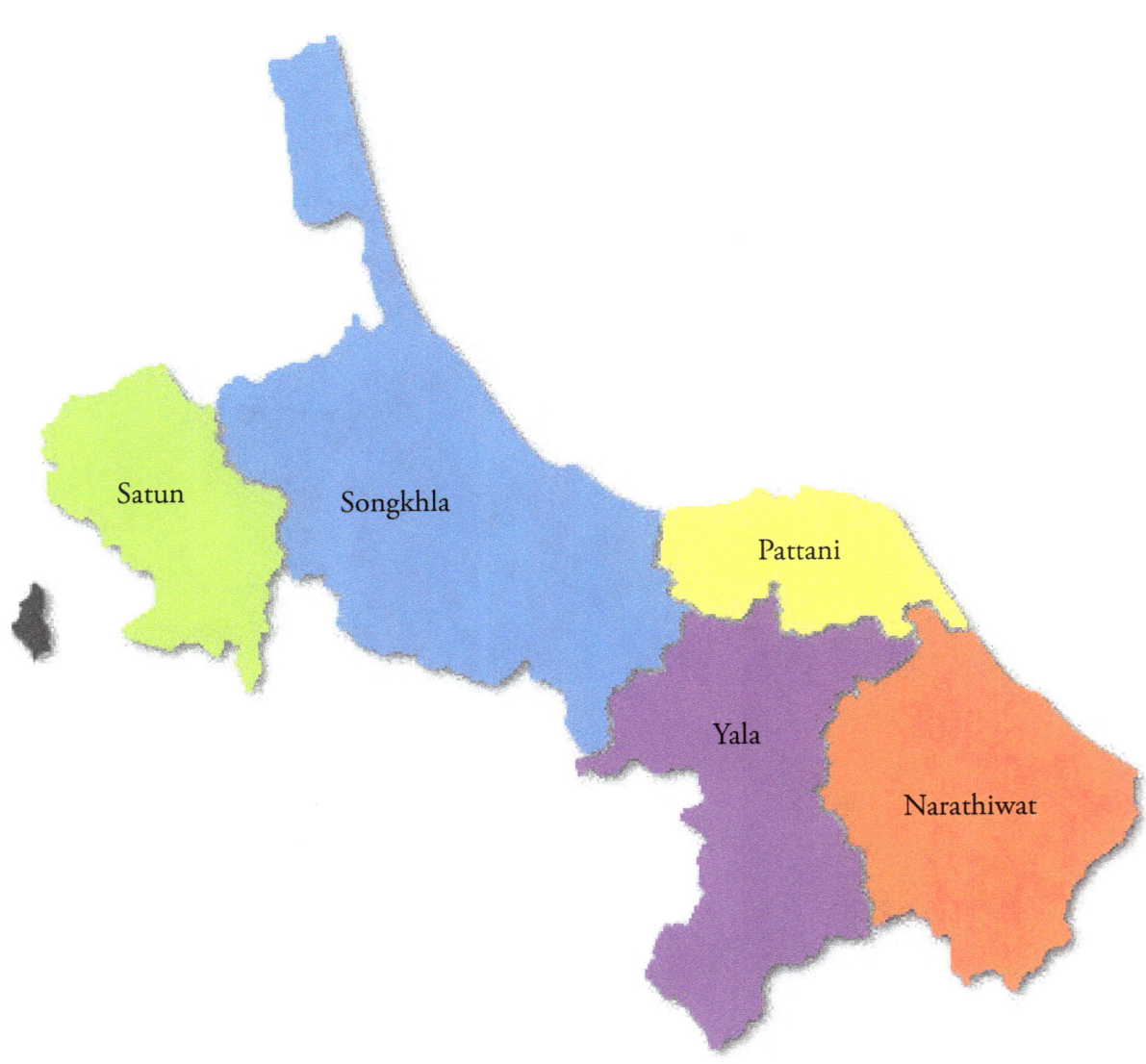

Map of the three southern border provinces

Bibliography

1. The Royal Thai Army. (2014, January 2). *10th anniversary of the southern violence.*

2. Wichai. (n.d.). *South strategy.* Retrieved from http://www.geocities.ws/wichai_cgucherd/southstragy.html

3. International Herald Tribune. (2007, June 14). Police say bomb at soccer match in Southern Thailand wounds 14 officers.

4. Ratchaikitcha. (n.d.). Retrieved from http://www.ratchaikitcha.soc.go.th/DATA/PDF/2548/00167632.PDF

5. China Economic Net. (n.d.). Army Commander's powers to rise: Thai Deputy PM.

6. Knowledge Surveillance Center. (n.d.). *Southern Situation Southern Situation Database.*

7. Issara News Institute, Journalist Association of Thailand Peace Media Project. (n.d.). *Southern News Desk.*

8. Southern Newspaper. (n.d.). *News and images of the South that are deeper and more extensive than other daily newspapers.*

9. Online Manager. (n.d.). *Open the Deep Southern Files.*

10. Bangkok Business Newspaper. (n.d.). *10 Southern crisis with pictures.* Retrieved from Bangkok Business Newspaper website.

11. Pattani Today. (n.d.). *Southern fire news.*

12. CNN. (n.d.). *News.*

13. Muslim Lawyers' Center & Volunteer Network of Legal Assistants. (n.d.). *Legal assistance in the three southern border provinces.*

14. (n.d.). *The Liberation Tiger Army of Thailand.*

15. Narasajja. (2005). Ethnic issues in Sri Lanka. *Journal of History, Srinakharinwirot University,* 79–106.

16. Soonsiri, L. C. P. (n.d.). *War of Terror... Danger Imminent.*
17. Independent Committee for National Reconciliation: KOSB. (n.d.). *Stop the Southern Fire.*
18. Council on Foreign Relations. (n.d.). *Background information on the Tigers.*
19. International Crisis Group. (n.d.). *Information on the conflict.*
20. Duncanson, D. (1966). *Government & revolution in Vietnam.*
21. (2004, December). *The official and personal diary in the field research.*
22. Post Publishing PLC. (2014, November). RKK member killed in Narathiwat. *Bangkok Post.*
23. Pike, J. (2014, November). Gerakan Mujahideen slam Pattani (GMPIP) – Global security.
24. Pattani Post. (2011, February 19). PULO and Mujahideen Forces.
25. (2009, April 18–19). PULO President invited to speak at OIC Meeting.
26. (n.d.). Neojihadism and YouTube: Pattani militant propaganda dissemination and radicalization.
27. (2014, November 28). Bomb blast in Pattani misses Aree.
28. The Nation. (n.d.). Shattered by horrific events. *Nationmultimedia.com.*
29. The Nation. (2004, April). Retrieved November 3, 2011.
30. The Nation. (2004, April). Southern carnage: Kingdom shaken. *Nationmultimedia.com.* Retrieved November 3, 2011.
31. Asian Centre for Human Rights. (n.d.). Killings at Pattani's Krue Se Mosque and a cover-up enquiry. *Countercurrents.org.* Retrieved November 3, 2011.
32. DPA. (n.d.). Thai Prime Minister throws cold water on peace talks plans.
33. (2006, May). *[Untitled source, inferred as a news report].*
34. The Nation. (2004, May 26). Negotiation talks: Separatists being overplayed.
35. The Nation. (2006, September 7). Leave the door open for talks.
36. (n.d.). Thailand modifying Muslim SOB-AKA.
37. The Nation. (n.d.). Sonthi calls for talks.
38. The Bangkok Post. (n.d.). Sonthi slams meddling.
39. Thai Deputy PM. (2006, September 8). Army Commander's powers to rise. *En.ce.cn.* Retrieved November 3, 2011.
40. The Bangkok Post. (2006, November 19). Deep South: Army wants talks but unsure who with.
41. The Nation. (2006, June 25). Prem disagrees with proposed use of Malay as official language. *Nationmultimedia.com.* Retrieved February 19, 2011.

42. Southern Border Provinces Administrative Centre. (2013, January 4). Cited in ISRA News report.

43. Fuller, T. (2009, April 31). Muslim insurgents confound military in Thailand. *The New York Times*. Retrieved February 19, 2011.

44. Bangkok Post. (2014, November 30). South violence enters 9th year! *Bangkok Post Opinion*.

45. Patani Post. (2014, October 14). Seven injured in explosion near hospital in Southern Thailand. *PataniPost.net*.

46. Human Rights Watch. (2007, August 27). No one is safe. *Hrw.org*. Retrieved November 3, 2011.

47. Human Rights Watch. (n.d.). Thailand beheading, burnings in renewed terror campaign. *Hrw.org*. Retrieved October 14, 2014.

48. Human Rights Watch. (n.d.). Thailand: Rebels escalate killings of teachers. Retrieved November, 2014.

49. MSNBC. (2006, January 8). Wave of attacks in Thailand. Retrieved February 19, 2011.

50. BBC News. (2005, November 3). Thai districts impose martial law. Retrieved May 23, 2010.

51. Council on Foreign Relations. (2007, February 1). The Muslim insurgency in Southern Thailand. Retrieved November 3, 2011.

52. Bangkok Post. (2011, June 4). Prayuth sees foreign hands plotting separatist violence. Retrieved November 3, 2011.

53. McCargo, D. (2008). *Tearing apart the land: Islam and legitimacy in Southern Thailand*. Cornell University Press.

54. Sugunnasil, W. (2006). Islam, radicalism, and violence in Southern Thailand: Berjihad di Patani and the 28 April attacks. *Critical Asian Studies, 38*(1), 119–144.

55. Jitpiromsri, S., & Sobhonvasu, P. (2006). Unpacking Thailand's Southern conflict: The poverty of structural explanations. *Critical Asian Studies, 38*(1), 95–117.

56. Storey, I. (2007, March 15). Malaysia's role in Thailand's southern insurgency. *Terrorism Monitor, 5*(5).

57. Office of National Economic and Social Development Board (NESDB). (n.d.). Poverty gap, poverty severity, poverty line, proportion of poor people and number of poor people (in terms of expenditure or consumption), 2533–2547.

58. Human Rights Watch. (n.d.). *No one is safe – The ongoing insurgency in Southern Thailand: Trends in violence, counterinsurgency operations, and impact of national politics* (p. 23).

59. Giglio, M. (2011, January 14). Thailand tries to project normality. *Newsweek*. Retrieved November 3, 2011.

60. AFP. (2011, March 7). Thailand says southern unrest worsening. Retrieved November 3, 2011.

61. Abuza, Z. (n.d.). *The ongoing insurgency in Southern Thailand*. INSS, p. 20.

62. Aphornsuvan, T. (n.d.). *Rebellion in Southern Thailand: Contending histories.*

63. Aphornsuvan, T. (n.d.). *Rebellion in Southern Thailand: Contending histories* (ISBN 978-981-230-2), p. 35.

64. The Royal Gazette. (1939, August 7). *Vol. 56*, p. 1281. Retrieved June 4, 2010.

65. Montesano, M. J., & Jory, P. (Eds.). (n.d.). *Election and political integration in the lower south of Thailand*, by Ockey, J. In *Thai South and Malay North: Ethnic interactions on a plural peninsular* (ISBN 978-9971-411-1), p. 131.

66. Umar, U. H. (n.d.). The assimilation of the Bangkok-Melayu communities.

67. Human Rights Watch. (n.d.). A brief history of insurgency in the southern border provinces. Retrieved November 28, 2014.

68. The Jamestown Foundation. (n.d.). A breakdown of Southern Thailand insurgent groups. *Terrorism Monitor, 4*(17). Retrieved November 28, 2014.

69. Gunaratna, R., & Acharya, A. (n.d.). *The terrorism threat from Thailand: Jihad or quest for justice?* Potomac Books. ISBN 978-1597972024.

70. Bangkok Post. (2008, August 4). Beheadings raise tensions in Thailand; Religion of Peace alert. Retrieved July 17, 2015.

71. (2010, May 26). Strategic insights – Unrest in South Thailand: Contours, causes, and consequences since 2001. *Ccc.nps.navy.mil*. Retrieved February 19, 2011.

72. Human Rights Watch. (n.d.). Thailand separatists: Targeting teachers in South. Retrieved November 28, 2014.

73. Human Rights Watch. (n.d.). Thailand beheadings, burnings in renewed terror campaign. *Hrw.org*. Retrieved November 14, 2014.

74. Human Rights Watch. (n.d.). It was like suddenly, my son no longer existed: Enforced disappearances in Thailand's southern border provinces. *Hrw.org*. Retrieved November 3, 2010.

75. International Business Times UK. (n.d.). Thailand policeman's wife shot dead and set on fire in revenge attack. Retrieved October 14, 2014.

76. Adams, B. (2010, January 20). Thailand: Serious backsliding on human rights. *Human Rights Watch*. Retrieved February 19, 2011.

77. Asian Human Rights Commission. (n.d.). Emergency decree legalize torture chambers.

78. The Nation. (2006, December 18). Group seeks asylum in M'sia alleging harassment by army.

79. The Nation. (2007, March 19). Military abused us, say fleeing Muslims.

80. Bangkok Post. (2012, November 30). Rangers killed civilians. *Bangkok Post News*.

81. Nanuam, W. (2015, August). Engagement of Malaysia and Indonesia on counterinsurgency in the South of Thailand. *Asia Pacific Center for Security Studies* (PDF). Archived from the original on September 29, 2015. Retrieved September 29, 2015.

82. University Malaysia Sarawak. (2013). *Southern Thailand peace talks: The long and winding road – Analysis* (PDF). Archived from the original on September 29, 2015.

83. Melbourne Law School. (2008). *Conflict in Southern Thailand* (PDF).

84. Nanuam, W. (n.d.). Panlop to face trial for the storming of Krue Se Mosque. *Seasite.niu.edu*. Retrieved November 3, 2011.

85. Nanuam, W. (n.d.). Security conflicts erupt in open. *Seasite.niu.edu*. Retrieved November 3, 2011.

86. The Nation. (2006, October 28). Wipe the Tak Bai slate clean.

87. The Nation. (2006, November). PM Sorayuth issues apologies for Tak Bai Massacre.

88. Chalk, P. (2008). *The Malay-Muslim insurgency in Southern Thailand: Understanding the conflict's evolving dynamic*. RAND National Defense Research Institute. ISBN 9780833045348.

89. Global Security. (n.d.). Thailand Islamic insurgency. Retrieved December 6, 2014.

90. International Crisis Group. (2005, May 18). *Southern Thailand insurgency, not jihad* (Asia Report No. 98) (PDF). Retrieved December 6, 2014.

91. Heenan, P., & Lamontagne, M. (2001, January). *The Southeast Asia handbook* (p. 176). Taylor & Francis. ISBN 978-1-884964-97-8.

92. Jones, D. M., & Smith, M. L. R. (2006). *ASEAN and East Asian international relations: Regional delusion* (p. 65). Edward Elgar Publishing. ISBN 978-1-84542-892.

93. Lewis, G. (2007, May 7). *Virtual Thailand: The media and cultural politics in Thailand, Malaysia and Singapore* (p. 175). Routledge. ISBN 978-1-134-21766-3.

94. Institute of Southeast Asian Studies. (2005). *Southeast Asian affairs*.

95. University of Central Arkansas. (n.d.). *Thailand/Malay Muslims (1948–present)*. Retrieved August 30, 2015.

96. (2014, July). *South Thailand security report*. Retrieved November 28, 2014.

97. International Herald Tribune. (2009, March 29). Police say bomb at soccer match in Southern Thailand wounds 14 officers. Retrieved November 3, 2011.

98. Bangkok Post. (2014, October). 27 wounded as 3 blasts hit Songkhla tourist area. Retrieved October 2014.

99. Janes.com. (2007, November 19). Mid-November 2007 update on the insurgency.

100. AFP. (2008, March 19). Bloodshed part of daily life in Thailand's Muslim South. *Afp.google.com*. Retrieved November 3, 2011.

101. Google News. (2010, February 2). Thailand can quash insurgency by year-end: Minister. Retrieved November 3, 2011.

102. Wikimedia Commons. (n.d.). *Media related to South Thailand insurgency*.

Note: Some of these websites may be censored for internet access from within Thailand:

- History of Jihad Thailand
- Daily collections of news about the southern insurgency
- Red Light Jihad: Thailand's new breed of Facebook Jihadis.
- Red Light Jihad: Insurgency in Thailand party town.
- Thailand Islamist Insurgency with NO End
- Thailand's secessionist Muslim Insurgency escalates
- Thailand Islamic Insurgency

Author's biography

Dr. Sompong Dumdeang

The author was ordained as a novice for the first time at Wat Pangtri. He studied Khmer language, astrology, fortune telling, chanting Abhidhamma sermons, Mahachat, Malay verses, and Buddhist traditions for 1 year. After that, he went to study Pali grammar and Dhammapada at Wat Sam Bo. After that, he moved to study Dhamma and Pali and became a first-class Dhamma scholar. and became a novice monk at Wat Huapom in Songkhla Province. After that, the writer went to study Pali at the highest level at Mahachulalongkornrajavidyalaya University, a Buddhist University in Bangkok. He resided at Wat Mai Phiren, Thonburi, Thailand.

In the time when the author studied at Mahachulalongkornrajavidyalaya University, the Buddhist Sangha of Thailand, the author was elected as the president of the university. One of the most important roles at that time was to raise funds to help the university. He was also appointed as the head of the university. Editor of the magazine "Siang Tham" of the university. At present, this Buddhist university offers doctoral degrees to both laypeople and monks in many fields of study.

The author graduated from the Faculty of Southeast Asia and was assigned by the former Chairman of the Committee of the Supreme Patriarch, Somdej Phra Phutthachan, "Kiew Upaseno", Wat Srakes Ratchaworamahawihan, Bangkok during the time when he was the Rector of that Buddhist University, to be the first Dharma Missionary to train and teach the people and monks in the northern provinces, especially the base of practice. Work at Khao Kho, Phetchabun Province by teaching Thai language, psychological issues related to religion and culture, both in terms of behavior to hill tribe people, including teaching them about health, learning how to cut their hair according to the United Nations project, and being a leader in attracting hill tribe youth to ordain and practice Buddhism at Wat Benchamabophit, Bangkok in large numbers. The author is interested in all hill tribes, but pays special attention to the Hmong hill tribe because he is interested in their language. He writes words every day. Later, the Ministry of Interior, through the Department of Public Welfare, published it as a document for reference. After the Hmong hill tribe immigrated to America, the author was one of the people who became the main figures in providing information. Help them get an education and give them a new and better life through the Department of Education in the Education Service Area under the English as a Second Language program. He has been fighting for legal rights for both hill tribes and Asian immigrants, including Americans, for more than a decade.

The author used to teach Dhamma at Wat Mahathat and Bang Khae Elderly Home, Bangkok. He used to be a Dhamma lecturer on the Border Patrol Radio Station in the program "Dhamma for the People." After that, he went to study in India for 2 years in the field of archaeology at Varanasi University. He received a Fulbright scholarship to study at universities in the United States. Both Harvard University and Washington University offered him to study. But the author decided to continue his studies at Washington University and was invited to lecture at leading universities in the United States and many other countries around the world.

In addition to being a university lecturer, the author is also the chairman and founder of International Cleaning Services, Inc. and American Asian International Contractor, which helped Indonesians flee the war into America after the Vietnam War and has also helped immigrants from all over the world. Until receiving the Outstanding Performance award, the company achieved the highest success in its operations until it was elevated to the status of a Federal Partner from former President George H.W. Bush of the United States.

The author is also a lawyer by establishing the Office of Lawyers for the Disadvantaged and has served as a cultural liaison between Americans and people from other countries around the world. The author has played an important role in matters related to Buddhism, culture, and national security in both the East and the West since the time of Princess Poonpismai Disakul, by bringing the philosophy and beliefs of Buddhism to teach and train millions of people, and create motivation for them to live their lives with purpose to achieve a better and happier life on this planet.

The author has been honored as a World Health Organization (WHO IS WHO) by People Magazine in America as a sociologist. He has also been a media representative and an editor for an Asian newspaper. The author is a true democrat. Learn and understand deeply

In the philosophy of both Western and Eastern philosophy, there is a long-lasting love and connection with pets. Once, the writer was shocked and deeply saddened by the passing of two pets: a beloved pitbull dog named Boo Boo and a cat named Sammy. He currently has pets that are like family members, namely an Aussie Pitbull named Rama and two Taos named Tata and Tootoo. Animal Pet Companion magazine wrote about him as a man who loves pets with a soul that is hard to compare.

When free from teaching, writing, and arguing, in terms of politics, economics, and society, the writer is happy working with his rice and garden, and spends some of his time traveling to every place in the world as much as the opportunity allows. The author had the opportunity to bring his American wife to meet the Pope in Rome, Italy in 2004 and was also honored by him to discuss Dharma in both Buddhist and Christian philosophies.

The author has established a charitable foundation under the laws of the United States. The author serves as both the founder and the CEO of the Dumdeang Foundation. The head office is located at 1138 S.E., Reynold Street, Portland, Oregon 97202, USA.

His Holiness Phra Phrom Khunabhorn (or as he is known as His Holiness Panya Nanta) on the occasion of his presiding over the opening ceremony of the Thai temple in America, he has called the writer in front of Thai people in America and Americans that Dr. Sompong Dumdeang is a progressive Thai who has established The foundation was established in America to help the underprivileged and the writer is one of his close students.

The Black and Red Foundation has played an important role in helping society. For example, when the tsunami hit Thailand in December 2004, the foundation, together with the US government, helped the victims of the tsunami by helping to set up hospitals and Clinics are set up to help the underprivileged in Sri Lanka and India in collaboration with the governments of both countries.

Although the author has settled in America for more than 50 years, the author has always loved and felt connected to his hometown. Whenever the opportunity arose, the author would return to visit Thailand and take the opportunity to visit his relatives, brothers and sisters, most of whom live in Songkhla and Satun provinces. However, this time, he also had an additional purpose. The author wanted to return to Khao Kho, an area that was once a forbidden territory for the general public during the year 1968, which was a place of communist terrorism to divide the country. The author at that time was appointed by the Thai Sangha as a representative. He was the first Dharma Ambassador to help the hill tribes to spread the religion to the hill tribes in order for them to return to cooperate with the government again. In addition, the author received a scholarship from the British Columbia University of Canada to write a research report on hill tribes in Thailand to the university and is still in the process of completing it completely.

The author studied Arabic and Persian at Washington University for more than 3 years. He collaborated with Dr. Nicolas of the Department of Oriental Languages to conduct a comparative study and develop a study of the concept of Buddhism on the topic of "Nirvana and Sufism" in Islam as the world of the intellect, which has crossed the level of traditional belief, which is not a contradiction. Contradicting the way of belief in Buddhism, which is the way to Nirvana, both Professor Dr. Nicolas and the writer agree that the way to Nirvana in Buddhism and Sufism in Islam are phenomena that are integrated both in philosophy and politics of both religions, which emphasize the truth and the truth that must be It is true to human life that this issue itself shows that conflict will never occur at the level of Sufism. Therefore, both the author and the co-author have tried to bring the concept to the Muslim world that our world has already moved beyond conflict, race and injustice.

The author volunteered as a member of the Office for Emergency Management, an agency of the United States government, also known as FEMA. Established during the time of President Jimmy Carter of the United States, the primary function of the agency is to coordinate the response to natural disasters occurring in various parts of the United States.

The proudest writer who has helped the society by donating money to build hospitals, nursing homes in India and clinics in Sri Lanka. He is the founder and chairman of the "Dumdeang Foundation" in the United States. To help the general community in every country Around the world, he was appointed as the team leader of the Northwest Medical Team to help victims of the 2004 Tsunami in Asia and returned to commemorate the event again in December 2005 to bring clothes, medicine and education funds from the Red Cross Foundation. Including the donation from the religious organization Good Samaritan to Thailand, Indonesia, Sri Lanka.

The author is a well-known author of many books on philosophy and Buddhism, as well as a number of historical, social and religious articles, such as:

1. Buddhist Philosophy A dissertation written for submission to the Graduate School of British Columbia University of Canada, Canada, for the degree of Doctor of Philosophy.

2. 21st Century BUDDISM

3. In 1980, he wrote an article about Buddhist monks and mountain people, called "Buddhist Monk and Mountainous People" in English, for use as a study guide for students at Washington University.

4. Guide to the Constitution of Life, published in Thailand in 2005

5. The Crisis of Conflict in 3 Southern Border Provinces of Thailand, co-written with Inthrakiat Rodpradit, the author is the main author.

The author has been honored by the United States Court of Justice as an Associate Judge. The main duty assigned by the Court is to jointly judge cases on criminal and social issues.

After the Vietnam War ended, people from Vietnam, Cambodia, Laos, and other parts of the world flocked to America in large numbers to find work and settle down. Those who entered America needed to receive care from the American government in terms of education, society, and medical care. There is one principle in which doctors provide medical care to foreigners. These immigrants must be able to communicate with each other in order to prevent medical professionals from being prosecuted for miscommunication with patients. The author has been helping immigrants in America for many years and has been appointed as official interpreters in various hospitals by the Supreme Court of America.

In addition to being a writer, the writer is also a reporter for several local newspapers. He has been a regular reporter for the Asia Reporter of Portland, Oregon, USA for many years. His reporting focuses on social, crime and religious issues until he was appointed as an editor.

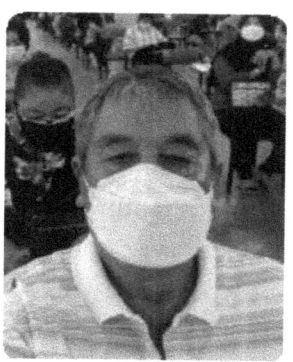

Intarakiat Rodpradit

Intarakiat Rodpradit graduated with a Bachelor of Commerce in Finance and Banking from the University of the Philippines in 1969 Studied distance learning with Alexander Hamilton Institute in New York City, USA in 1972 in the course of "Modern Business Management". Was once assigned to the US Air Force Base at Korat during the Vietnam War but later withdrew and started working In the international affairs department of the first Thai commercial bank, he was the first head of the international business center of that commercial bank before joining the oldest French commercial bank (Sog:Gen) that invested in Thailand as the director of international trade business in 1997 for 3 years before resigning to do his own business.

The author has been appointed as an advisor to the chairman of the Senate's Subcommittee on Economics, Finance and Banking (Dr. Pa Aksornsue) and has been an advisor to many master's degree students in many leading Thai educational institutions that offer international master's degree programs that stipulate the conditions in the early days that students who will graduate from the master's degree program His master's degree required him to present his thesis in English. This led him to become both a translator and a writer.

In addition, the author has been a lecturer on international trade at leading financial institutions in Thailand, including the Department of Export Promotion, Ministry of Commerce, and has been invited to be a special lecturer on international trade at the University of the Thai Chamber of Commerce.

The author was once assigned to the US Air Force Base at Korat during the Vietnam War for a short period of time, after which he was withdrawn. He reported to a leading financial institution in Thailand in 1969 for some historical benefit. The author briefly explains that the United States came to establish a base in Thailand to send aircraft to attack northern Vietnam. During the Vietnam War, there were 6 US air bases in Thailand: Don Mueang Air Base, Khorat Air Base, Nakhon Phanom Air Base, Okat Takli Air Base, Ubon Air Base, and Udon Air Base. The author passed the written test and interview from the intelligence unit in Bangkok to enter. Working at the US Air Force Base in Korat

The most exciting thing is refusing to cooperate with the criminal gang. Plan to cheat the bank by offering him 12 million baht in cash just to agree to cooperate in forging the guarantee contract. Or a promissory note that will be issued to a commercial bank in the amount of 100 million baht (one hundred million baht) at the time he worked at a leading commercial bank.

The most exciting thing is escaping an attack by armed pirates in the southern part of Negros Oriental, Philippines. It happened around 1967 when a Filipino friend who was a His classmates invited him to go on vacation on his family's private island with his family. In preparation for the battle against the pirates' armed forces, weapons of war were distributed to everyone. His biggest problem at that moment was that he had never shot a gun in his entire life. The university he was studying at did not allow him to shoot. Foreign students studying the course of national defense in such a situation He asked for only a short gun. He survived by luck.

Interested in history, translation and writing.

As a translator, he has translated books from Thai to English, such as the history of the Malay Kingdom of Pattani, called "Kingdom of Pattani". He has translated many books from English to Thai, such as the biography of Father David E. Weekley, the story in the wilderness, "In From the Wilderness", etc.

As a writer, I became a co-author of the book. "Crisis...Conflict in 3 Southern Border Provinces" was invited by Dr. Sompong Dumdeang, the main writer of this book, to travel to America for 90 days at the end of the year 2014 and wrote a book called "Two Friends Adventuring on the American Land: My Life and 90-Day Experience" And this book is distributed nationwide by Kledthai Company Limited.

www.ingramcontent.com/pod-product-compliance
Lightning Source LLC
Chambersburg PA
CBHW080521030426
42337CB00023B/4589